A TASTE OF
HOME

The Ballyknocken Cookbook

A TASTE OF
HOME

The Ballyknocken Cookbook

Catherine Fulvio

GILL BOOKS

Gill Books

Hume Avenue

Park West

Dublin 12

www.gillbooks.ie

Gill Books is an imprint of M.H. Gill & Co.

978 07171 7260 3

Designed by Jane Matthews

Photography by Harry Weir and Brian Clarke

Food styling by Sharon Bradford

Edited by Emma Dunne

Proofread by Fiona Biggs

Indexed by Adam Pozner

Printed by L.E.G.O. S.p.A, Italy

PROPS

Meadows and Byrne: (01) 280 4554, www.meadowsandbyrne.ie

Strawbridge, Mount Usher Gardens: (0404) 40502, www.strawbridge.ie

Ballyknocken Cookery School: (0404) 44672, www.ballyknocken.com

This book is typeset in Tarocco.

The paper used in this book comes from the wood pulp of managed forests.
For every tree felled, at least one tree is planted, thereby renewing natural resources.

A CIP catalogue record for this book is available from the British Library.

5 4 3 2

DEDICATION

✦

To all generations of the Byrne-Fulvio family at Ballyknocken, especially to my mother, Mary, and my father, Charlie. You are the foundations, whose love of this magical and beautiful piece of Irish countryside and whose hard work has built Ballyknocken to what it is today.

May the future generations enjoy it as much as we have.

ACKNOWLEDGEMENTS

✦

So here's my sixth book and it is the one closest to my heart. It has captured the essence of Ballyknocken: our past, our present, our hopes and dreams for the future. I have so many people to thank for getting me and Ballyknocken to this point.

To my lovely children Charlotte and Rowan, and to all my friends and family, most especially my dad, Charlie. Thank you for your wonderful support. No matter what, you are always there for me.

In particular, a very special thanks to Sharon and Daniel who did a fantastic job cooking and styling the food for the photographs. Your support has been invaluable.

To the amazing Harry and to Brian, our hugely talented photographers, it's always a pleasure to work with you – guaranteed great photos and a bundle of laughs as well.

To all of my colleagues here at Ballyknocken House & Cookery School, especially Sharon, Gema, Jolita, Virga, Ciaran, Ann and Aoife. Your dedication is hugely appreciated. It's my pleasure to work with such talented people.

To the team at Gill, especially Nicki, Deirdre, Sarah, Catherine, Teresa, Emma L. and Emma D., Fiona, Brid and Paul, thank you for your vision, encouragement and support. Thanks to Emma and Fiona for all of their editing work. And to our fantastic designer, Jane, you see beauty in what I see every day – thank you for your creativity and beautiful design.

CATHERINE FULVIO

BALLYKNOCKEN HOUSE, FARM & COOKERY SCHOOL

Catherine Fulvio is the proprietor of Ballyknocken House & Cookery School, County Wicklow, and one of Ireland's top television culinary stars. Her previous books, *Catherine's Italian Kitchen*, *Catherine's Family Kitchen*, *Eat Like an Italian, Bake Like an Italian* and *The Weekend Chef*, were all bestsellers. Born and raised in Ireland and married to an Italian, Catherine's books always reflect this match-made-in-heaven by using easily accessible Irish ingredients assembled with Italian flair. Catherine also appears on ABC's *Today Show USA* and BBC1's *Saturday Kitchen*.

CONTENTS

1

INTRODUCTION

✣

5

RISE & SHINE
The Ballyknocken Breakfast

How to ... Cook Eggs 6
My Childhood Porridge with Cinnamon and Pear Compote 10
Orchard Apple Breakfast Compote 12
Rhubarb, Orange and Ginger Compote 14
Ballyknocken Granola 18
'In a Rush' Smoked Bacon and Broccoli Frittata 19
Spinach Fritters with Poached Eggs and Roast Tomatoes 20
Ballyknocken Drop Scones with Blackberry Sauce and Orange Mascarpone Cream 22
French Toast with Rose Petal Syrup, Plums and Goat's Cheese 24

✣

29

SIMPLE BEGINNINGS
Easy Starters

The Ballyknocken Irish–Italian Antipasti platter 31
Scotch Egg Salad with Tarragon Mayonnaise, Rocket and Chargrilled Asparagus 37
Smoked Trout, Dill and Strawberry Salad 38
Crab and Dillisk Mini-Tartlets 40
Chargrilled Prawn Skewers with Marie Rose Sauce 41
Chicken Liver Parfait 42
Easy Mackerel Pâté 44
Roasted Red Pepper, Leek and Soft Farmhouse Cheese Terrine 46
Cheesy Lemon Cups with Garlic Herb Oil 50
Smoked-Salmon Roll Salad 52
Tomato, Yoghurt and Lemon-and-Chilli Pesto Pots with Flattened Toasted Herb Ciabatta 54

57

FARMHOUSE SOUPS

My Favourite Soups

How to ... Make Great Vegetable and Chicken Stock *58*
Duo of Soups – Beetroot and Jerusalem Artichoke with Bacon *60*
Sorrel, Wild Garlic and Potato Soup *62*
Curried Mussel Soup *64*
Shallot, Spinach and Barley Soup *66*
Kale, Cannellini and Potato Soup *68*

71

FRESH CATCH

Fish Mains

How to ... Cook Fish *72*
Tomato Haddock with Asparagus and Prosciutto *76*
Baked Trout with Fennel, Lime and Wasabi Cream Sauce *78*
Smoked Salmon and Salmon Fish Cakes *79*
Baked Oysters with Bacon *82*
The Murrough Posh Fish Pie *84*
Irish Seafood Risotto *86*

89

OF PASTURES FAIR

Meaty Mains

How to ... Cook Meat *90*
Herby Parmesan-Encrusted Rack of Wicklow Lamb with Plum Salsa *94*
Leg of Wicklow Lamb with Moroccan Mint Jelly and Shallot and Red Wine Gravy *96*
Lamb Wellington with Wild Garlic *100*
Wicklow Lamb Steak with Wild Leaves, Mushrooms and a Blackberry Dressing *102*
Chicken Supreme with Spinach and Herb Stuffing and Sorrel Cream Sauce *104*
Italian-Style Tomato, Shallot and Rosemary Chicken Hotpot *106*
Sicilian Lemony Roast Chicken and Potatoes *108*
Wicklow Wolf Braised Beef *110*
Beef and Stout Pies with Potato Pastry Topping *112*
Peppered Sirloin Steak with Whiskey Cream Sauce *115*
Rosemary, Apple and Celery-Stuffed Pork Chops with Apple Cider Sauce *116*
Stuffed Date and Hazelnut Pork Fillet with Creamy Mushroom and Pink Peppercorn Sauce *118*
Ham Croquettes with Leek and Paprika Sauce *120*
Rosemary Venison with Shallot and Red Wine Sauce *122*
Five-Spice Seared Duck Breasts with Honey and Raspberry Sauce and Wilted Pak Choi and Spring Onions *124*
Winter Rabbit Casserole *126*

129

THE GREAT VEG PLOT
Sides and Salads

How to ... Make the Most of Vegetables *130*
Ballyknocken Dauphinoise *134*
Mustard and Spinach Mash *135*
Garlic and Rosemary Roast Potatoes *136*
Polenta and Parsley Chunky Parsnips *138*
Cauliflower Cheese Bake *140*
Honey, Red Wine and Juniper Red Cabbage *141*
Purple Sprouting Broccoli with Wild Garlic Sauce *144*
Pan-Fried Rainbow Chard with Garlic and Blue Cheese *146*
Beetroot and Prosciutto Salad with Orange Dressing *148*
Mint, Artichoke and Broad Bean Salad with Herb Dressing *150*
Chargrilled Courgette Salad with Crumbled Black Pudding and Chilli Sauce *151*
Mangetout, Wicklow Blue Cheese and Borage Flower Salad with Strawberry Dressing *154*
Shallot and Pear Tarte Tatin *156*
Individual Tomato and Basil Summer Puddings *158*

161

FRESH FROM THE GARDEN
Accompaniments and Preserves

How to ... Plant a Micro Herb Garden *162*
Herb Syrups *166*
Chocolate Mint Liqueur *168*
Catherine's Favourite Pesto *169*
Herb Salts *170*
How to ... Make Great Jam *172*
Strawberry and Balsamic Jam *176*
Apple Jelly *178*
Ballyknocken's Famous Rhubarb and Ginger Jam *179*
Cinnamon Pear Preserve *180*
Plum and Red Onion Chutney *182*
Marsala Pear Relish *183*

185

ON THE SWEETER SIDE
Cakes and Desserts

Mary's Eve's Pudding with Lemon Verbena Cream 186
Elderflower Fritters 187
Chocolate Mousse Cake 188
Very Berry Pannacotta Tart 190
Mini Strawberry and Lemon Éclairs 192
'The Perfect Fools' – Gooseberry and Elderflower and Blackcurrant and Rosemary 194
'To Die For' Lemon Meringue Pie 198
Prosecco, Lemon Balm and Blueberry Jellies 200
Blackberry and Rhubarb Upside-Down Cake 202
Wicklow Summer Pudding 204

207

HARVEST TIMES
Breads and Baking

Ballyknocken Soda Seed Bread 208
Soda Farls 209
Mary's Brown Bread 210
Lemonade, White Chocolate and Fraughan Scones 212
Caramelised Onion and Leek Scones 216
Oaty Chive Biscuits 217
Aunty Trina's Tea Brack 218

221

CHURN IT UP
Milk and Cheese

How to ... Make Yoghurt and Butter 222
Three Flavoured Butters 224
Three Yoghurt Dressings 225
Apricot and Lemon Balm Yoghurt Cake 226
A Celebratory Cheese Cake 228
Cheeseboard Essentials 230

233

FARMHOUSE FESTIVITIES

Christmas at Ballyknocken

Ballyknocken Bay, Thyme and Cranberry Christmas Turkey with Bacon Stuffing Balls *234*
Festive Baked Ham *238*
Individual Black Forest Trifles *242*
Ginger and Orange Christmas Pudding *244*

250

INDEX

INTRODUCTION

THE STORY OF BALLYKNOCKEN HOUSE & COOKERY SCHOOL

❈

I look back romantically on my time growing up here on the farm at Ballyknocken House. Doesn't everyone think the same of their childhood? I don't remember a single drop of rain any summer. I recall long days of golden sunshine as we played in the hay fields till late into the evening. There was real snow in the winter, sufficient to ensure a week off school while we made a sled from the bonnet of a VW Beetle and hurtled down the hills of the farm at high speed. When I see my children nowadays with all their electronics for amusement, my childhood seemed positively wild, fun filled and packed with energy.

But of course there was plenty of hard work and trauma too – the hens scared the living daylights out of me! They nested in boxes about five feet off the ground, so when I was sent out to collect the eggs, I had to stand on my tippy toes and reach in. It was always a gamble as to whether there was a hen still nesting in the box, as I couldn't see in, being too small. Invariably the hens would take flight in my direction, annoyed at being disturbed – very scary for a six-year-old!

So if you've never been on a farm before, here are some tips based on my experiences:

- Never attempt to enter a field where there's a cow with a calf – even if you can run very, very fast!

- Don't practise your driving in a field where there's a bull. Those L-plates really hold you back!

- If a loved one asks you to make fresh butter, pray that there's a machine involved, because turning the handle of a milk churn by hand for hours is not fun for a seven-year-old – or someone of any age for that matter!

- If you are asked to help pluck turkeys, hope that plural means no more than two. The problem with turkey plucking is that there's a specific deadline called Christmas Day, so the pressure will be on.

- When you are asked to help pick a few turnips, be warned that that means a few fields, not just two or three turnips!

- Moving sheep from one field to another doesn't necessarily mean that the fields are beside each other – there could be a six-mile gap and a forest between them!

But one thing I can assure you of is that growing up on the farm here at Ballyknocken really was a perfect childhood! I loved feeding the baby calves and lambs, milking the cows, planting and harvesting in the fruit and vegetable gardens and my grandparents' orchard. I thoroughly enjoyed driving the tractor when bringing in the hay from the fields – although I was fired from that duty after I let my foot off the clutch too quickly and all the boys fell off the trailer at the back. It can be dangerous growing up on a farm, especially with me around!

But what I really relished was the time in the kitchen with my mother. Mum opened our farmhouse as a B&B in 1969 and cooked three meals a day for guests, most of whom stayed for a minimum of a week. The food was freshly made for each meal and the menu varied daily. So from a very young age, I learned what fresh food was all about and I also learned how to be creative in cooking. There was never any food waste, as we understood the value of food and the hard work that goes into its production. We ate, and still do eat, by the seasons.

My mother was very hard-working and entrepreneurial. When the B&B closed in the winter, she would take to rearing turkeys for the Christmas market. She was also the queen of gadgets – always looking for a new way to present dishes or speed up the preparation process. For example, she came home one day and proudly displayed her new purchase – a pineapple peeler. It was impossible to buy a pineapple in our county at the time, but we were ready for action with our peeler whenever they would become available! But most of all she loved to cook – it was by hanging on to her apron strings that I honed my skills, and we are still a B&B to this day, cooking dinner for resident guests at the weekends.

Our farmhouse was built in the 1850s for the local land agent. For all of my childhood there has been a huge rusty pot filled with flowers outside. Dad thought that his father used this pot to cook potatoes for the pigs. But, more recently, we discovered that it was a famine soup pot. And here we are still making soups for visitors to this day at Ballyknocken.

Our children are the fourth generation here at Ballyknocken Farm, and I can trace my family back to the early 1800s as farmers and landowners in the locality. So there is a clear history of production from the land – and my mother and I took it to the next level of 'farm to fork'. In 2003 I converted the old milking parlour that my grandad built into Ballyknocken Cookery School – I so enjoy teaching there, sharing knowledge, tips and stories and simply having fun being creative with ingredients, many of them local, and making delicious dishes.

And not only are we proud of our Irish heritage but we also have an Italian mix, as my Sicilian husband and his family have brought their passion for fresh food and their love of all things Mediterranean to our welcoming table. This cookbook is a mix of modern Irish food with farm-to-fork principles, peppered with Italian influences and some nostalgic recipes from my childhood. It's a food story from our farm, our B&B and our cookery school here at Ballyknocken, nestled in the gentle rolling hills of Glenealy in the beautiful Garden of Ireland, County Wicklow. It is our Taste of Home.

Warmest wishes from the farm and kitchens of Ballyknocken House,

RISE
&
SHINE

The Ballyknocken Breakfast

When my mother started the B&B back in 1969 I tagged along behind her, and cooking breakfast was the first thing I learned. I loved working alongside my mum and was never short of jobs. If I wasn't collecting eggs from the hen house, I was juicing oranges or setting tables, and eventually I was promoted to cooking breakfast – and serving it! For me, breakfast is a special meal and it's important that we begin our day with good, local produce that we know the origins of. Nowadays, after breakfast our guests attend cookery classes, go on lengthy hikes, go biking, visit the beautiful gardens here, like Mount Usher, or head for the beach. So ensuring that before they start they have time to sit down, be pampered a little and enjoy country-style hospitality is what I aim for. Balancing their energy requirements with pleasure in the food is top of my list for good menu planning.

How to …
COOK EGGS

Recently our hen house was home to Martha, Mabel, Mags, Myrtle, Miriam and Matilda – it was designed so that the ladies had plenty of space to run around. My colleagues took turns to feed them, and we all became quite attached. Mabel was my favourite (yes, I had a pet hen) – she would rush up to me when she saw me. I'm fairly sure her motives were only food driven, but I like to think that she thought we were besties! Sadly, as we live so close to the amazing Carrick forest, which seems to be home to Ireland's main fox population, we struggled to keep our hens safe. So now our wonderful local farmer provides us with his very tasty free-range eggs.

BOILED

Please don't laugh because I'm giving you tips on how to boil an egg – it's a basic but invaluable skill! Use free-range eggs wherever you can and make sure they are at room temperature before you start. Fill a saucepan with plenty of water – enough to cover the eggs when added. Bring the water to the boil, then reduce the heat to a simmer. Add the eggs and give them a gentle stir – this sits the yolk in the middle of the egg.

The following timings are for large eggs.

SOFT: simmer for 3 minutes – the white is solid and the yolk runny: ideal for dipping 'soldiers'.

MEDIUM: simmer for 4½ minutes – the yolk is solid but still moist and orange/yellow in colour.

HARD: simmer for 7 minutes – the yolk is solid, light yellow and crumbly: good for picnic eggs and in salads.

When the eggs are cooked to your liking, take them out of the saucepan using a slotted spoon.

SCRAMBLED

For me, the key here is a non-stick saucepan or small frying pan. For a single serving, melt 1 tbsp butter in the pan and add 2 tbsp milk. Meanwhile whisk 2 eggs in a small bowl. When the butter is melted and the milk warm, add the whisked eggs to the pan. Let them settle for about 30 seconds then start to 'scramble' with a non-stick spatula or wooden spoon. When they begin to set but still have a creamy texture, the eggs are ready. Lightly season with salt and freshly ground black pepper and serve immediately – scrambled eggs can't wait: they have to be enjoyed as soon as they're made.

FRIED

For the classic Irish fry you need a perfect fried egg – they are very popular in our B&B. Heat 2 tsp butter and 1 tsp rapeseed oil in a non-stick frying pan over a medium heat. Crack the egg into the pan if you're feeling confident, or break it into a cup first and then carefully slide it into the pan. Reduce the heat and cook for about 2 minutes, until the white is set and the yolk is set on the outside and a little soft in the centre. If you want an 'over easy' egg, flip it and cook for 1 minute on the other side.

POACHED

Ah, now this is my favourite, especially in Eggs Benedict. You could try the little poaching cups you can buy, but for me that's a gadget too far! Simply fill a medium saucepan two-thirds with boiling water and add 1 tsp of white wine vinegar and a little salt. Return the water to the boil then stir it and add the egg into the vortex. The vortex and vinegar will keep the egg white together. Reduce the heat and simmer for about 3 to 3½ minutes until cooked to your liking. A trendy way to poach eggs is to pour the egg into clingfilm, twist it tightly shut, then submerge it in boiling water for about 3 minutes.

OMELETTES

THE EASY WAY OUT

For each omelette, you'll need 2 eggs, 1 tbsp butter, salt and freshly ground black pepper and your choice of filling (see below). Make sure you have everything ready before you start.

Break the eggs into a bowl and whisk very well with a fork. Add the butter to a medium non-stick frying pan over a medium heat and heat the butter until it bubbles. Add the egg mixture and swirl evenly. Leave to settle for about 1 minute then, using a thin spatula, lift the edges up, allowing the uncooked egg to run under. Cook for a further 1 minute and then add the filling. Season with salt and freshly ground black pepper. Once the egg has set, fold the omelette in half and slide onto a warm plate to enjoy immediately.

THREE EASY AND DELICIOUS FILLINGS

The Mediterranean: 2 tbsp chopped sundried tomatoes, a good handful of rocket leaves, about 2 tbsp local soft goat's cheese and chopped parsley, with plenty of freshly ground black pepper on top

The Leftovers: 3 tbsp chopped home-cooked ham, 5 small steamed broccoli florets (I keep cooked florets in my fridge for convenience), about 3 tbsp chopped roasted red peppers (which I also keep in my fridge) and ½ tsp chopped oregano

The Spanish: shredded raw spinach, grated local mature Cheddar and a few tbsp of finely chopped chorizo, which I crisp up first and then add

My Childhood Porridge with Cinnamon and Pear Compote

Serves 2

Anyone who has lived on a farm understands the heartiness of steaming hot porridge after an early morning start milking the cows. I love mine with fruit. To keep the pears in the compote from browning, I add lemon juice, which also gives that sharp lift I love.

FOR THE COMPOTE

This serves 3 to 4 – it's great to have some left over to spoon over yoghurt!)

120G CASTER SUGAR

250ML WATER

1 CINNAMON STICK

5 LARGE PEARS, PEELED, CORED AND DICED

1 LEMON, ZEST AND JUICE

FOR THE PORRIDGE

100G PORRIDGE OATS

PINCH OF SALT

150ML MILK

100ML WATER

1 TBSP FINELY CHOPPED DRIED APRICOTS

PINCH OF CINNAMON

HONEY, TO DRIZZLE

To prepare the compote, place the sugar, water and cinnamon stick in a saucepan. Bring to the boil, then simmer until a light syrup has formed. This will take about 7 to 8 minutes. Add the diced pears, lemon zest and juice and simmer slowly for about 10 minutes until the pears are just softened. Leave to cool completely, then remove the cinnamon stick. Spoon into a sterilised jar (see p. 133) and seal well.

To make the porridge, put the porridge oats and a pinch of salt into a large saucepan, add the milk and water and place over a medium heat, stirring until the porridge thickens. Then stir in the chopped apricots and a pinch of cinnamon and cook for a further 2 minutes. Add a little more water or milk if you feel that the porridge is too thick, and stir again.

To serve, ladle the porridge into two warm bowls, spoon over some of the pear compote and top with a swirl of honey.

The pear compote will keep in the fridge for 10 to 14 days.

ORCHARD APPLE BREAKFAST COMPOTE

Makes about 1kg

Our orchard is abundant with beautiful juicy apples. And neighbours and friends who have an oversupply often leave boxes of apples at our kitchen door. (Thank you so much for doing this – you know we put them to good use!) Using different apple varieties makes for a great compote.

5 BRAMLEY APPLES, PEELED, CORED AND DICED

3 PINK LADY APPLES, PEELED, CORED AND DICED

250G CASTER SUGAR

¼ TSP GROUND CINNAMON

60ML COLD WATER

1 LEMON, ZEST AND JUICE

5 WHOLE CLOVES AND 1 STAR ANISE, WRAPPED IN A MUSLIN CLOTH, TIED WITH A LONG STRING

Place the diced apples, sugar and ground cinnamon in a large saucepan over a medium heat.

Pour in the water, lemon zest and juice. Add the clove-and-anise bag and simmer slowly for about 15 to 18 minutes, until the apples are just softened.

Remove the bag and leave the compote to cool completely before spooning into a bowl or a sterilised jar (see p. 133) ready for the fridge, where it will keep for about 2 weeks.

Neighbours and friends who have an oversupply often leave boxes of apples at our kitchen door.

RHUBARB, ORANGE AND GINGER COMPOTE

Makes about 1kg

I have a soft spot for rhubarb. And here's a gardener's tip: it is so easy to grow! Rhubarb suits both savoury and sweet and is delicious with meats or, in this case, for breakfast.

1 TBSP MELTED BUTTER

1KG RHUBARB STALKS, TRIMMED AND CUT INTO 4CM LENGTHS

150G CASTER SUGAR

50G SOFT BROWN SUGAR

½ TO ¾ TSP GROUND GINGER

depending how strong a ginger flavour you like

1 MEDIUM ORANGE, ZEST AND JUICE

Preheat the oven to 180°C/fan 160°C/gas 4. Brush a shallow roasting tray with the melted butter.

To start with, place the rhubarb lengths into the roasting tray and spoon over the caster sugar, brown sugar and ground ginger. Then toss the rhubarb and sugars together. Sprinkle half of the orange zest and all of the juice over the top and place in the oven for about 12 to 15 minutes until the rhubarb is lightly caramelised and has just softened but still holds its shape.

Remove from the oven, cool completely, then add the rest of the orange zest and carefully mix. Transfer to a bowl, cover with clingfilm and place in the fridge until ready to use. It will also keep in a sterilised jar in the fridge for up to 2 weeks.

BALLYKNOCKEN GRANOLA

Makes about 600g

From the day I took the reins at our farmhouse B&B I started to make granola. It's so tasty and versatile. Layering homemade granola between thick natural yoghurt and sliced strawberries, or any berries of your choice, in pretty glasses for brunch is not only delicious but looks gorgeous.

2 TBSP SUNFLOWER OIL

4 TBSP HONEY

350G PORRIDGE OATS

100G QUINOA FLAKES

3 TBSP SUNFLOWER SEEDS

4 TBSP SESAME SEEDS

3 TBSP PUMPKIN SEEDS

2 TBSP PISTACHIOS, ROUGHLY CHOPPED

4 TBSP DESICCATED COCONUT

2 TBSP RAISINS

2 TBSP DRIED CRANBERRIES

Heat the oven to 180°C/fan 160°C/gas 4. Line a large baking tray with parchment paper.

To prepare the granola, mix the oil and honey in a large bowl. Add the remaining ingredients, except the coconut, raisins and cranberries, and mix well.

Pour this mixture onto the lined baking tray and spread evenly. Bake for 18 to 20 minutes, stirring from time to time to help brown evenly.

Mix in the coconut, raisins and cranberries and bake for a further 5 minutes. Keep an eye on it, as it can quickly burn around the edges.

Remove from the oven and leave to cool completely before spooning into a storage jar.

'In a Rush' Smoked Bacon and Broccoli Frittata

Serves 4

Don't be discouraged if your frittata doesn't unmould neatly the first time you make it – the trick is a good quality ovenproof non-stick frying pan! Once you get the hang of them, frittatas will be your go-to midweek supper dish. If there are any leftovers, I pack them for school lunches or even take some with me on the road as a substantial snack.

EXTRA VIRGIN OLIVE OIL

100G SMOKED BACON, CUT INTO LARDONS

6 SPRING ONIONS, FINELY SLICED

2 TSP CHOPPED THYME

6 LARGE FREE-RANGE EGGS

1 TSP CHOPPED PARSLEY

PINCH OF NUTMEG

4 TBSP GRATED PARMESAN

SALT AND FRESHLY GROUND BLACK PEPPER

12 SMALL FLORETS STEAMED BROCCOLI

GENEROUS HANDFUL WATERCRESS LEAVES MIXED WITH 1 TBSP CHOPPED PARSLEY, TO GARNISH

Heat some oil in an ovenproof frying pan over a medium heat. Add the bacon lardons and sauté until cooked and crispy. Transfer to a clean plate.

Wipe out the pan with kitchen paper and heat a little more oil in it. Add the spring onions and thyme and sauté on a low heat for about 5 minutes until the spring onions are soft and lightly caramelised. Using a slotted spoon, lift them from the pan and discard the remaining oil.

In a large bowl, mix together the eggs, parsley, nutmeg, Parmesan, salt and freshly ground black pepper. Add the broccoli, spring onions and smoked bacon to the egg mix and stir well.

Add a little more oil to the pan. When hot, pour in the frittata mixture and cook over a low heat until the egg begins to set.

Preheat the grill to a medium heat. Once the frittata has set around the edges but is still liquid in the middle, transfer the pan to under the grill. Cook for about 5 minutes, until the centre is just set and golden. Be careful, as the pan handle may be hot!

To remove the frittata from the pan, run a small palette knife around the edge of the pan, place a large plate over it and invert the pan. The frittata should gently pop onto the plate. Then place another plate over the frittata and invert again, so the presentation side is up.

To serve, place a handful of watercress and parsley in the middle of the frittata. Slice into wedges and enjoy.

Spinach Fritters with Poached Eggs and Roast Tomatoes

Serves 2, makes 6 medium

Spinach goes incredibly well with poached eggs, and we have plenty in the garden, so using spinach that is picked on the day makes this even more special.

FOR THE TOMATOES

10 CHERRY TOMATOES ON THE VINE, WASHED

2 GARLIC CLOVES, SLICED

5 SMALL SPRIGS OF BASIL

OLIVE OIL, FOR DRIZZLING

SALT AND FRESHLY GROUND BLACK PEPPER

FOR THE FRITTERS

100G PLAIN FLOUR

1 TSP BAKING POWDER

½ TSP PAPRIKA

SALT AND FRESHLY GROUND BLACK PEPPER

1 FREE-RANGE EGG, BEATEN

50ML MILK, YOU MAY NEED A LITTLE MORE

LARGE HANDFUL SPINACH LEAVES, FINELY CHOPPED

OLIVE OIL, FOR FRYING

FOR THE POACHED EGGS

2 LARGE FREE-RANGE EGGS

SALT

1 TBSP WHITE WINE VINEGAR

1 BAY LEAF

SPRIGS OF BASIL, TO GARNISH

Preheat the oven to 180°C/fan 160°C/gas 4. Line a roasting tray with parchment paper.

Place the tomatoes, garlic slices and a few sprigs of basil into the tray. Drizzle over some oil and season with salt and freshly ground black pepper. Roast in the preheated oven for 18 to 20 minutes, carefully turning from time to time. Remove the tomatoes from the oven, snip them into clusters of 2 or 3, keeping them on the vine, and keep warm.

To prepare the fritters, mix the plain flour, baking powder, paprika, salt and freshly ground black pepper together in a medium bowl. Combine the egg and milk in a jug. Stir the egg mixture into the dry ingredients until a smooth, thick batter forms. Check the consistency – the batter should drop easily from the spoon. If it's too wet, add a tablespoon or so of flour; if it's too thick, add a little milk. Then stir in the chopped spinach.

Heat a small amount of oil in a large non-stick frying pan over a medium heat and spoon the batter into the oil – roughly 2–3 tbsp per fritter. Cook for about 1½ minutes on each side until cooked through. Remove to a large plate lined with kitchen paper and keep warm.

To poach the eggs, fill a small saucepan two-thirds with boiling water, add a little salt, the vinegar and the bay leaf. Bring to the boil. Crack an egg into a cup. Stir the boiling water to form a vortex and then carefully add the egg to it. Do the same for the next egg. Reduce the heat slightly and poach for about 3 to 4 minutes.

For each serving, pile 3 fritters onto a warm plate and spoon the roasted cherry tomatoes around. Place a poached egg on top and sprinkle a little coarsely ground black pepper over it as well as some basil sprigs.

Ballyknocken Drop Scones with Blackberry Sauce and Orange Mascarpone Cream

Serves 2, makes 6 small

Drop scones are the most popular breakfast served here at the B&B. We are often asked for the recipe so here it is for you. I hope you enjoy them as much as we do!

FOR THE SAUCE

2 TBSP HONEY

75ML ORANGE JUICE

4 TBSP BLACKBERRIES

4 SMALL SPRIGS OF THYME

FOR THE ORANGE MASCARPONE CREAM

1 ORANGE, ZEST ONLY

3 TBSP ICING SUGAR

100ML CREAM

100ML MASCARPONE

FOR THE DROP SCONES

100G PLAIN FLOUR

1 TSP BAKING POWDER

2 TBSP GROUND ALMONDS

1 TBSP SUGAR

100ML BUTTERMILK

1 LARGE FREE-RANGE EGG, BEATEN

40G MELTED BUTTER

SUNFLOWER OIL, FOR FRYING

SPRIGS OF THYME, TO GARNISH

To make the sauce, combine the honey and orange juice in a medium saucepan and simmer for 4 to 5 minutes until a light syrup forms. Add the blackberries and sprigs of thyme, remove from the heat and leave to cool.

Whisk all the ingredients for the orange mascarpone cream together well and place in the fridge until you're ready to serve.

To make the drop scones, sift the flour and baking powder into a medium-sized bowl. Add the ground almonds and sugar. Stir in the buttermilk, beaten egg and melted butter and whisk until a smooth, thick batter is formed. Leave to stand for 5 minutes before using. If it is then too thick to drop easily from a spoon, add a tablespoon or two of water.

Heat a little oil in a large non-stick frying pan over a medium heat. Spoon about 2–3 tbsp batter per scone into the pan – you might need to cook them in batches. When bubbles appear on the tops of the drop scones, carefully turn them over and cook on the other side until golden. Remove from the pan and keep warm.

To serve, place 2 drop scones on each plate beside each other and another on top, and spoon the blackberry sauce over them.

Decorate with sprigs of thyme, spoon over some orange mascarpone cream and serve immediately.

Breakfast is a special meal and it's important that we begin our day with good, local produce.

French Toast with Rose Petal Syrup, Plums and Goat's Cheese

Serves 2

Poached plums and local McDonnell's goat's cheese are two yummy ingredients that team together beautifully when serving French toast for brunch. If you don't fancy goat's cheese, try crispy bacon.

FOR THE SYRUP

100G CASTER SUGAR

120ML WATER

10 ORGANIC ROSE PETALS

FOR THE PLUMS

2 PLUMS, STONES REMOVED AND SLICED IN WEDGES

SMALL BUNCH OF REDCURRANTS

FOR THE FRENCH TOAST

2 LARGE FREE-RANGE EGGS

60ML MILK

1 TBSP ICING SUGAR

PINCH OF CINNAMON

BUTTER, FOR FRYING

4 SLICES BRIOCHE LOAF (STALE WORKS BEST)

50G SOFT GOAT'S CHEESE, TO SERVE

EDIBLE VIOLAS, TO DECORATE

To make the syrup, place the sugar and water in a medium saucepan over a high heat. Bring to the boil and then reduce the heat. Simmer for about 8 minutes until a light syrup forms. Remove from the heat and add the rose petals. Leave to cool completely and then remove the petals. The syrup will keep in the fridge for 2 weeks.

To poach the plums, add the plum wedges and redcurrants to a small saucepan over a low heat, pour in about 4 tbsp of the cooled rose syrup and cook for 3 to 4 minutes. Set aside.

To make the French toast, whisk the eggs, milk and icing sugar together in a large shallow dish. Mix in the cinnamon. Heat a little butter in a large non-stick frying pan over a medium heat. Using a fork, dip both sides of each piece of brioche into the egg mixture and carefully place in the frying pan. You might need to do this in batches, depending on the size of your pan. Cook until lightly golden on both sides.

Using a spatula, transfer the French toast to a serving plate, arrange the plum wedges and redcurrants on top, spoon over some syrup and add small spoonfuls of cheese. Decorate with edible violas and serve immediately.

Anyone who has lived on a farm understands the heartiness of steaming hot porridge after an early morning start milking the cows.

SIMPLE BEGINNINGS

Easy Starters

In our cookery school, I'm often asked to suggest easy and doable starters. I like to begin with a salad using my favourite garden leaves, poached pears or plums, hazelnuts and an artisan blue cheese, or a smoked salmon salad with lime dressing and mango slices. I try to add to my five a day everywhere! I always say, keep starters simple and you will have a winner. Choose local ingredients that most people will feel comfortable eating, and make the dishes ahead of time if you have a complicated main to cook. It's no use stressing yourself over a dinner party – life is way too short for that! Dinner parties are for relaxing and enjoying good company. But don't forget that we also eat with our eyes so presentation is important too. A little drizzle of herb oil over steamed vegetables is good, or orange zest on fish (a zester with channel knife will help you to be creative), or a small bunch of bay and dill tied with thin string sits well on the side of a pretty platter of salmon. Edible flowers are easy to grow and look beautiful too.

CAPONATA

LEMON HUMMUS

FIG AND OLIVE
TAPENADE

ONION, LEEK AND
PANCETTA TART

THE BALLYKNOCKEN IRISH–ITALIAN ANTIPASTI PLATTER

Serves 6 to 8

This is the starter board that we serve to resident guests for dinner on Friday and Saturday evenings. It's inspired by my trips to Italy but uses our wonderful local produce and the vegetables grown in our own garden. We are always asked for the recipes during the cookery class the morning after.

SICILIAN CAPONATA
Makes about 750g

FOR THE HOMEMADE TOMATO SAUCE (MAKES 750ML)

50ML EXTRA VIRGIN OLIVE OIL

3 GARLIC CLOVES, FINELY CHOPPED

1 TSP TOMATO PURÉE

800G TINNED WHOLE PLUM TOMATOES, CRUSHED

SALT AND FRESHLY GROUND BLACK PEPPER

SUGAR

FRESH BASIL LEAVES

FOR THE CAPONATA

1 LARGE AUBERGINE, CUT INTO 2CM DICE

SALT

EXTRA VIRGIN OLIVE OIL

1 LARGE ONION, CHOPPED

2 CELERY STICKS, TRIMMED AND CUT INTO 1.5CM PIECES

500ML HOMEMADE TOMATO SAUCE

3 TBSP CAPERS, RINSED

4 TBSP WHITE WINE VINEGAR

SUGAR, TO TASTE

100G GREEN OLIVES

FRESHLY GROUND BLACK PEPPER

First make the tomato sauce. Heat the olive oil in a large pan. Add the garlic and cook for about 1 minute on a low heat until soft. Add the tomato purée and cook for a further minute. Add the tomatoes with their juice and season with salt and freshly ground black pepper. Bring to the boil, reduce the heat and simmer for about 30 minutes or until the sauce has thickened. Adjust the seasoning, adding sugar, salt and freshly ground black pepper to taste, and then add the basil. The sauce will keep in the fridge for 1 week and can be frozen for months.

Next, degorge the aubergine by placing the diced aubergine pieces in a colander and sprinkling with salt. Leave for 30 minutes to allow the bitter juices to drain, then rinse well and pat dry.

Heat some olive oil in a deep frying pan and shallow fry the aubergines until they are soft and golden. Drain on kitchen paper and set aside.

Heat some more olive oil in a saucepan and sauté the onion and celery on a low heat for 7 to 10 minutes, until they begin to colour. Add the tomato sauce, capers, vinegar and sugar, then simmer for 5 minutes.

Add the cooked aubergine and olives, then simmer for 10 minutes. Check the seasoning, adding salt and freshly ground black pepper as needed.

Allow to cool and refrigerate for 24 hours before serving at room temperature with crusty bread.

FIG AND OLIVE TAPENADE
Makes about 400g

150G DRIED FIGS, CHOPPED

4 TBSP BRANDY

200ML WATER

125G PITTED BLACK OLIVES

5 ANCHOVY FILLETS

1½ TBSP CAPERS, DRAINED

½ LEMON, JUICE ONLY

1 TBSP DIJON-STYLE MUSTARD

100ML EXTRA VIRGIN OLIVE OIL

SALT AND FRESHLY GROUND BLACK
PEPPER, TO TASTE

Place the figs, brandy and water in a small saucepan and simmer for about 10 minutes until the figs are soft.

Then put the poached figs, olives, anchovies, capers, lemon juice and mustard in a food processor and blend to a thick paste. With the machine running, gradually pour the olive oil in a thin, steady stream through the feed tube to make a thick spread. Check the seasoning, adding salt and freshly ground black pepper if needed.

LEMON HUMMUS
Makes about 300g

250G COOKED CHICKPEAS (CANNED
ARE FINE – JUST RINSE WELL)

1 SMALL LEMON, ZEST AND JUICE

3 TBSP TAHINI PASTE

1 LARGE GARLIC CLOVE, THINLY SLICED

½ TSP GROUND CUMIN

¼ TSP CAYENNE PEPPER

50ML EXTRA VIRGIN OLIVE OIL

SALT AND FRESHLY GROUND BLACK
PEPPER

Place the chickpeas, lemon zest and juice, tahini paste, garlic, cumin and cayenne pepper in a food processor and blend until smooth.

While the machine is running, pour in the extra virgin olive oil to form a textured paste, adding more oil if a looser hummus is preferred.

Check the seasoning, adding salt and freshly ground black pepper as needed.

BALLYKNOCKEN GARDEN SALAD
WITH LEMON AND BALSAMIC DRESSING
Serves 6

FOR THE DRESSING

1 LARGE LEMON, JUICE
AND ZEST

120ML EXTRA VIRGIN OLIVE
OIL

2 TSP LOCAL HONEY

2 TSP FINELY CHOPPED
CHIVES

1 TSP WHOLEGRAIN
MUSTARD

1½ TBSP BALSAMIC
VINEGAR

SALT AND FRESHLY
GROUND BLACK PEPPER

FOR THE SALAD

200G OF YOUR FAVOURITE
LETTUCE LEAVES

*We would include
(depending on the season)
mizuna, rocket, red oak,
red sails, frisée, radicchio,
lamb's leaf, lolla rossa –
washed and torn*

GENEROUS HANDFUL
CELERY LEAVES, WASHED

4 RADISHES, SLICED

10 SMALL SPRIGS OF
PARSLEY, WASHED

10 SMALL SPRIGS OF DILL,
WASHED

10 EDIBLE BORAGE
FLOWERS

To make the dressing, put the lemon juice and zest, oil, honey, chives and mustard into a small bowl and whisk well. Add the balsamic vinegar and whisk again. Check the seasoning: you may need to add a little more lemon juice or honey depending on the acidity levels. Season with salt and freshly ground black pepper and set aside.

To assemble the salad, place the leaves and radish slices into a bowl and spoon some dressing over them. Add the parsley and dill sprigs with the borage flowers.

✸✦✸

Onion, Leek and Pancetta Tart
Serves 10

FOR THE PASTRY

200G PLAIN FLOUR, PLUS
EXTRA FOR DUSTING

80G BUTTER, CHILLED AND
DICED

2 TBSP GRATED PARMESAN

1 TSP THYME, FINELY
CHOPPED

1 FREE-RANGE EGG YOLK

2 TO 3 TBSP CHILLED
WATER (YOU MAY NEED
LESS)

EGG WASH, TO GLAZE

FOR THE FILLING

RAPESEED OIL FOR
SAUTÉING

1 ONION, FINELY CHOPPED

½ LARGE LEEK, FINELY
SLICED

100G PANCETTA, DICED

3 FREE-RANGE EGGS, PLUS
2 FREE-RANGE EGG YOLKS

1 TBSP CHOPPED CHIVES

100ML CRÈME FRAÎCHE

150ML CREAM

SALT AND FRESHLY
GROUND BLACK PEPPER

100G SOFT GOAT'S
CHEESE

DILL AND BORAGE
FLOWERS TO DECORATE

Preheat the oven to 190°C/fan 170°C/gas 5. Brush a 23cm loose-based flan tin with melted butter. Dust with a little flour.

To make the pastry, sift the flour into a mixing bowl. Add the butter, Parmesan and thyme and rub into the flour until it resembles fine breadcrumbs. Add the egg yolk and enough water to form a firm dough. Wrap the dough in clingfilm and rest in the fridge for 30 minutes.

Then, on a floured surface, roll out the pastry until slightly larger than the tin. Line the tin with the pastry and trim the edges. Keep the trimmings to patch the tart after it has been blind baked. Place a circle of parchment paper over the pastry and fill with baking beans. Transfer to the oven and bake for 10 minutes. Remove the beans and paper, patch the pastry if required and brush with egg wash. Return to the oven for 5 to 6 minutes until lightly golden and glazed. Remove the pastry case from the oven.

Meanwhile, for the filling, heat the oil in a frying pan and sauté the onion and leek over a medium heat until soft and cooked through. Remove and set aside. Increase the heat and fry the pancetta until lightly crispy. Then place all the ingredients for the filling, except the goat's cheese, into a large jug and mix well. Season with salt and freshly ground black pepper. Carefully pour the filling into the pastry case and sprinkle the goat's cheese on top.

Bake for 20 to 25 minutes or until the filling is set. Serve warm or cold, garnished with dill.

TO ASSEMBLE THE PLATTER

To assemble the platter as a sharing starter, you'll need a large board. Arrange 6 to 8 slices of your favourite Italian and Irish charcuterie (bresaola, mortadella, coppa or prosciutto di Parma, as well as air-dried smoked Connemara lamb, wild boar and venison salami or spiced beef) on the board. Then spoon the caponata, tapenade and lemon hummus into small, pretty bowls. Place slices of the onion, leek and pancetta tart on the board as well as a generous amount of garden salad with lemon and balsamic dressing. Add in some breads and there you have a great starter. As a help-yourself starter, place each dish into a bowl on the table and arrange the cured meats on a board. Slice the tart and serve on a large platter with sprigs of basil in between. Divide the garden salad between two medium-sized bowls with the dressing in a jug so that everyone can tuck in.

Scotch Egg Salad
with Tarragon Mayonnaise, Rocket and Chargrilled Asparagus

Serves 4

My friends always said my mother was the Scotch-egg queen – little did they know it was me who had to make them! We would have them once or sometimes twice a week on picnics, for lunch when helping with the hay bales and even in our school packed lunch!

FOR THE SCOTCH EGGS

300G MINCED PORK

1 TSP CHOPPED SAGE

1 TSP CHOPPED THYME

1 TBSP FINELY CHOPPED PARSLEY

3 SHALLOTS, FINELY CHOPPED

SALT AND FRESHLY GROUND BLACK PEPPER

4 LARGE FREE-RANGE 7-MINUTE BOILED EGGS, SHELLED

4 TBSP PLAIN FLOUR, SEASONED WITH SALT AND FRESHLY GROUND BLACK PEPPER

1 FREE-RANGE EGG, BEATEN

50G BROWN BREADCRUMBS

SUNFLOWER OIL, FOR DEEP FRYING

FOR THE TARRAGON MAYONNAISE

4 GENEROUS TBSP HOMEMADE MAYONNAISE

4 TBSP CREAM

1 TSP FINELY CHOPPED TARRAGON

SALT AND FRESHLY GROUND BLACK PEPPER

FOR THE ASPARAGUS

200G ASPARAGUS SPEARS, TRIMMED AND SLICED LENGTHWAYS

RAPESEED OIL, FOR CHARGRILLING

FRESHLY GROUND BLACK PEPPER

7 SMALL SPRIGS OF THYME

GOOD HANDFUL ROCKET LEAVES, WASHED

To prepare the eggs, mix the minced pork with the sage, thyme, chopped parsley and shallots and season well with salt and freshly ground black pepper. Divide the meat into 4 equal portions and flatten into an oval large enough to wrap around each boiled egg. Dust each egg with the seasoned flour, then carefully wrap with the pork mixture.

Pour the beaten egg into a shallow bowl and spread the breadcrumbs onto a large plate. Dip the meat-wrapped eggs into the beaten egg and then in the breadcrumbs. Put on a clean plate and leave in the fridge to set for about 20 minutes.

Heat the sunflower oil to 150°C in a deep fryer or deep saucepan and add the eggs. Cook, turning every so often, until golden and lightly crisp and the pork is fully cooked through – about 4 to 5 minutes. Remove, drain on kitchen paper and keep warm.

To prepare the tarragon mayonnaise, mix all the ingredients together and check the seasoning before adding salt and freshly ground black pepper to taste.

For the asparagus, brush the spears with rapeseed oil and season with black freshly ground black pepper. Heat the chargrill pan over a medium heat and cook the spears for about 2 minutes on each side. Remove, sprinkle with sprigs of thyme and keep warm.

To make the salad, place the rocket leaves on a large serving platter with the asparagus spears on top. Slice the eggs in half, arrange on the asparagus and spoon the mayonnaise over.

Smoked Trout, Dill and Strawberry Salad

Serves 4

Many years ago we had a group of hillwalkers staying and my mother decided that she would treat them to Wicklow trout for dinner, so she asked Dad to order 40. Well, she nearly had a conniption when she arrived back from a day's shopping to find that 40 boxes had been delivered. Yes, we were now the proud owners of 400 trout! Anyone in the family who had a freezer had it stuffed full of trout for months!

FOR THE DRESSING

4 TBSP NATURAL YOGHURT

3 TBSP MAYONNAISE

½ LEMON, JUICE AND ZEST

1 TSP HONEY

3 TBSP WATER

SALT AND FRESHLY GROUND BLACK PEPPER

FOR THE SALAD

100G YOUR CHOICE OF LETTUCE LEAVES, WASHED AND TRIMMED

2 CELERY STICKS AND LEAVES, TRIMMED, SLICED ON THE DIAGONAL

150G STRAWBERRIES, HULLED AND SLICED

3 SMOKED-TROUT FILLETS, DEBONED AND ROUGHLY FLAKED

THIN LEMON WEDGES, TO GARNISH

7 TO 8 SMALL SPRIGS OF DILL, TO GARNISH

To make the dressing, mix all the ingredients together well. Season with salt and freshly ground black pepper – if it's too thick, add a little more water.

To assemble the salad, place the lettuce leaves and celery on a platter. Put the strawberries on top and spoon over a little of the dressing. Add the flaked trout and spoon over more dressing. Arrange the lemon wedges over the trout and, finally, top with the sprigs of dill. Serve immediately.

CRAB AND DILLISK MINI-TARTLETS

Makes 6

Highly popular in our superfood cookery class, as it is packed with nutrients, Dillisk (also known as Dulse) is a lovely red-coloured seaweed that we also use in baked egg dishes, yeast breads and even stir fries.

MELTED BUTTER, FOR BRUSHING

FLOUR, FOR DUSTING

FOR THE PASTRY

180G PLAIN FLOUR

100G CHILLED BUTTER

½ LEMON, ZEST ONLY

1 LARGE FREE-RANGE EGG YOLK, BEATEN

2 TBSP COLD WATER (YOU MAY NEED A LITTLE MORE)

EGG WASH

FOR THE FILLING

3 TSP FINELY CHOPPED DILLISK

2 TSP CHOPPED DILL

4 FREE-RANGE EGGS, BEATEN

300ML CREAM

SALT AND FRESHLY GROUND BLACK PEPPER

120G FRESH WHITE CRAB MEAT

Brush 6 loose-based 6cm tart tins with melted butter and dust with a little flour.

To prepare the pastry, place the flour, butter and lemon zest into a food processor and blend until the mixture resembles fine breadcrumbs. Add the egg yolk and sufficient water to form a soft dough.

Flour a clean surface and roll out the pastry. Cut 6 circles of pastry large enough to line the bottom and sides of each tin and carefully fit the pastry circles inside the tins. Place the tartlets on a baking tray and leave to rest in the fridge for 30 minutes.

Preheat the oven to 190°C/fan 170°C/gas 5.

Line each of the pastry cases with parchment paper and fill with baking beans. Bake for about 10 minutes, then check – they should be just baked and firm to the touch – and then remove the paper. Brush the pastry with egg wash and return to the oven for a further 5 minutes or until just golden.

To prepare the filling combine the Dillisk, dill, eggs and cream in a jug and season with salt and freshly ground black pepper. Divide the crab meat between the 6 tartlet cases and pour in the egg and cream mixture. Bake for about 18 to 20 minutes or until just set.

Leave to cool on a rack before removing from the tins. Serve with a green salad.

Chargrilled Prawn Skewers with Marie Rose Sauce

Serves 4, makes 8 skewers

I change these for the winter months by serving them with ginger mash and a warm spinach and orange salad with hot dressing rather than the Marie Rose sauce.

FOR THE MARIE ROSE SAUCE

2 LIMES, JUICE ONLY

4 TBSP TOMATO KETCHUP

1 TBSP WORCESTERSHIRE SAUCE

2 TO 3 DROPS TABASCO SAUCE

¼ TSP SMOKED PAPRIKA

5 TBSP MAYONNAISE

4 TBSP CREAM

SALT AND FRESHLY GROUND BLACK PEPPER

FOR THE PRAWN SKEWERS

1 GARLIC CLOVE, FINELY CHOPPED

1 LIME, ZEST ONLY

1 TBSP CHOPPED PARSLEY

2 TSP CHOPPED CHIVES

3 TBSP RAPESEED OIL

24 LARGE RAW PRAWNS, DEVEINED AND TAILS LEFT ON

16 CHERRY TOMATOES

2 LIMES, ONE CUT INTO 8 SLICES AND THOSE SLICES CUT IN HALF AGAIN, THE OTHER CUT INTO 4 WEDGES

16 SMALL BAY LEAVES OR KAFFIR LIME LEAVES

RAPESEED OIL, FOR BRUSHING

GEM LETTUCE LEAVES, TO GARNISH

2 TBSP TOASTED DESICCATED COCONUT, TO GARNISH

BUNCH OF CORIANDER, CHOPPED, TO GARNISH

If you are using wooden skewers, soak them in water for at least 2 hours before threading.

To make the sauce, combine all the ingredients and check the seasoning, adding salt and freshly ground black pepper to taste.

To prepare the prawns, first combine the garlic, lime zest, parsley, chives and oil in a shallow bowl to make a marinade. Pat dry the raw prawns if they're quite wet.

Onto each skewer, thread 3 prawns with cherry tomatoes, lime slices and bay leaves in between. Place them into the marinade and leave for 10 minutes.

Preheat a chargrill pan over a medium to high heat. Brush the skewers and the lime wedges with oil and chargrill for about 2 to 3 minutes before turning over and cooking for 1 to 2 minutes on the other side.

To serve, place the lettuce leaves onto a large platter and arrange the skewers on top with the chargrilled lime wedges.

Spoon over the Marie Rose sauce and sprinkle with the toasted coconut and fresh coriander.

Chicken Liver Parfait

Serves 4

I think there is nothing nicer in the winter months than a well-made chicken liver parfait with crispy bread as a snack while you toast your toes in front of the fire.

Here's a tip: taking the parfait out of the fridge 20 minutes before serving takes the chill off and enhances the flavours; serve with your favourite seed bread or even celery sticks.

120G BUTTER

1 MEDIUM ONION, FINELY CHOPPED

350G CHICKEN LIVERS, TRIMMED

1 TSP CHOPPED THYME

4 TBSP BRANDY

1/2 ORANGE, JUICE AND ZEST

1 TBSP WORCESTERSHIRE SAUCE

SALT AND FRESHLY GROUND BLACK PEPPER

FEW SMALL BAY LEAVES, WASHED

4 TBSP MELTED BUTTER

To make the parfait, melt the butter in a large frying pan over a medium heat and add the onion. Sauté for 6 minutes until softened but not browned.

Add the chicken livers, thyme and brandy and sauté for 4 to 5 minutes until the livers are just cooked. Remove from the heat and allow to cool a little.

Using a slotted spoon, transfer the cooked livers to a food processor. Add the orange juice and zest and Worcestershire sauce. Blend until smooth. Check the seasoning and add salt and freshly ground black pepper to taste. Spoon the parfait into small pots or ramekins. Allow to cool completely and place in the fridge to set.

Once set, place a bay leaf on top of each pot or ramekin, spoon over a little melted butter and return the parfaits to the fridge.

Serve each parfait with crusty bread and some Marsala Pear Relish (see p. 183).

EASY MACKEREL PÂTÉ

Serves 4

When I'm having a crowd around I also make a salmon version of this by poaching 2 salmon darnes and adding 6 cooked prawns instead of the mackerel.

250G SMOKED MACKEREL FILLETS

100G CRÈME FRAÎCHE

4 TBSP CREAM

2 TSP FINELY CHOPPED DILL

½ LEMON, ZEST AND JUICE

1 TBSP CHOPPED PARSLEY

2 SPRING ONIONS, FINELY CHOPPED

SALT AND FRESHLY GROUND BLACK PEPPER

CUCUMBER RIBBONS, TO SERVE

Carefully debone the mackerel fillets and place into a food processor. Add the crème fraîche, cream, dill, lemon zest and juice and parsley. Pulse just enough to form a roughly textured paste.

Stir in the chopped spring onions. Check the seasoning, adding a little salt and freshly ground black pepper as required. Spoon into a bowl, cover with clingfilm and place in the fridge until ready to serve.

To prepare the cucumber ribbons, slide a vegetable peeler along the length of a cucumber, shaving off thin slices.

To serve, place a pile of cucumber ribbons on a plate with a small ramekin of pâté and some crusty bread.

Roasted Red Pepper, Leek and Soft Farmhouse Cheese Terrine

Serves 4

I think the best way to serve this is to put the whole terrine in the centre of the table and let everyone dig in. It looks really impressive and is a definite crowd pleaser. Roasted peppers are delicious in salads or soups. The best way I know to peel them is to roast them at fan 200°C for 25 minutes until blistered and blackened and then place into a sealed plastic bag for about 10 minutes. Peeling them will be so easy.

EXTRA VIRGIN OLIVE OIL, FOR SAUTÉING

1 MEDIUM LEEK, SLICED IN HALF LENGTHWAYS

6 ROASTED RED PEPPERS, PEELED AND DESEEDED, EACH SLICED INTO 4

FOR THE FILLING

400G CREAM CHEESE

100G GREEK-STYLE NATURAL YOGHURT

4 TBSP PITTED BLACK OLIVES, CHOPPED

2 TSP CHOPPED OREGANO

½ LEMON, ZEST ONLY

1 TBSP CHOPPED PARSLEY

SALT AND FRESHLY GROUND BLACK PEPPER

FOR THE SALSA

10 CHERRY TOMATOES, FINELY DICED

6 PITTED BLACK OLIVES, SLICED

½ LEMON, ZEST ONLY

4 TBSP EXTRA VIRGIN OLIVE OIL

6 FRESH OREGANO LEAVES

SALT AND FRESHLY GROUND PEPPER

CRUSTY BREAD, TO SERVE

Heat a large frying pan with a little oil and lightly sauté the leeks. Leave to cool.

Place a doubled layer of foil 20cm long on a baking tray. Lay the pieces of red pepper in 3 adjoining rows along the length of the foil, just touching each other, and lay the leeks across all 3 rows.

To make the filling, combine the cream cheese, yoghurt, olives, oregano, lemon zest and parsley in a bowl. Season with salt and freshly ground black pepper to taste.

Spoon the cream-cheese mix on top of the leeks, piling it up slightly.

Fold the foil in on the two ends. Gather up the two long sides of the foil, fold over and seal. Smooth the sides and leave to set overnight in the fridge.

To make the salsa, mix all the ingredients together well, almost crushing them.

To serve, unwrap the terrine and place on a large board or pretty platter. Spoon the salsa over the top. Using a sharp knife, cut a few 5cm slices of terrine and serve with crusty bread.

I always say, keep starters simple and you will have a winner.

Cheesy Lemon Cups with Garlic Herb Oil

Serves 4

We love teaching Italian recipes in the cookery school and this one in particular reminds me of Sorrento, where I have enjoyed many delicious dishes, including lemon pasta served in large lemon shells. Inspired by the Amalfi Coast, this recipe is perfect for a starter.

4 LARGE LEMONS, HALVED

1 MEDIUM RED CHILLI, DESEEDED AND FINELY CHOPPED

100G GRATED PARMESAN

150G RICOTTA

100G TBSP PISTACHIO NUTS, ROUGHLY CHOPPED

100G MOZZARELLA, TORN

1 TSP OREGANO, CHOPPED

1 TSP ROSEMARY, CHOPPED

SALT AND FRESHLY GROUND BLACK PEPPER

2 TBSP PARSLEY, CHOPPED

8 TBSP BROWN BREADCRUMBS

FOR THE HERB OIL

100ML OLIVE OIL

2 GARLIC CLOVES, CRUSHED

50ML LEMON JUICE

4 TBSP CHOPPED MIXED HERBS SUCH AS DILL, THYME, ROSEMARY, PARSLEY AND OREGANO

SALT AND FRESHLY GROUND BLACK PEPPER

STRIPS OF LEMON ZEST, TO GARNISH

HANDFUL SPINACH LEAVES, SHREDDED, TO SERVE

To prepare the lemons, squeeze the juice from them and retain for the herb oil. Run a sharp knife between the skin and flesh of each lemon half and, using a spoon, scoop out and discard the flesh, then set the remaining skins aside.

Preheat the grill to medium.

Mix the chilli, Parmesan, ricotta, pistachios, mozzarella, oregano and rosemary, season with salt and freshly ground black pepper and spoon this cheese mixture into the empty lemon halves. Place in a medium-sized gratin dish. Combine the parsley and breadcrumbs and sprinkle over the lemon halves. Grill for about 5 minutes until the cheese is melted and the topping crisp.

To make the herb oil, pour the oil into a blender. Add the garlic and lemon juice and blend until smooth. While the motor is still running, add the herbs and blend. Check the seasoning, adding salt and freshly ground black pepper to taste.

To serve, put a handful of shredded spinach on each serving plate and place two lemon halves on top. Spoon over some herb oil, garnish with a sprig of rosemary or dill and serve immediately.

Smoked-Salmon Roll Salad

Serves 4

Our cookery students are always looking for quick and easy starters that can be prepared ahead. I'd highly recommend this recipe as it's oh-so easy, oh-so tasty – and always impressive!

FOR THE DRESSING

1 ORANGE, ZEST AND JUICE

100ML EXTRA VIRGIN OLIVE OIL

1 TSP CASTER SUGAR

1 TBSP CHOPPED DILL

SALT AND FRESHLY GROUND BLACK PEPPER

FOR THE SMOKED SALMON ROLLS

150G FIRM CREAM CHEESE

3 TBSP NATURAL YOGHURT

½ LEMON, ZEST ONLY

3 TBSP FINELY CHOPPED BLACK OLIVES

1 TBSP CHOPPED CAPERS

1 TBSP CHOPPED CHIVES

2 TSP CHOPPED DILL

SALT AND FRESHLY GROUND BLACK PEPPER

200G SLICED SMOKED ORGANIC IRISH SALMON

200G ASSORTED LETTUCE LEAVES, WASHED AND TRIMMED

4 RADISHES, THINLY SLICED

2 ORANGES, PEELED AND SLICED

4 TBSP CAPERS, DRAINED

To prepare the dressing, put the orange zest and juice in a small bowl, add the oil, sugar, dill, salt and freshly ground black pepper and whisk well. Check the seasoning, adding freshly ground black pepper and a little salt if needed.

To make the smoked salmon rolls, combine the cream cheese, yoghurt, lemon zest, olives, chopped capers, chopped chives and dill together. Season with salt and freshly ground black pepper. Then lay a piece of salmon flat on a plate, place a spoonful of the seasoned cream cheese at one end, roll up and set aside on a clean plate. Continue with all the salmon slices.

To assemble the salad, place the lettuce leaves, radish and orange slices and capers in a bowl, spoon over a little dressing and lightly toss.

Transfer the salad to a serving platter and then arrange the smoked-salmon rolls over the leaves. Serve the remaining dressing in a jug on the side.

TOMATO, YOGHURT AND LEMON-AND-CHILLI PESTO POTS
WITH FLATTENED TOASTED HERB CIABATTA

Makes 6 small pots/jars

This is the Italian flag in a jar! It's a fun starter that's easy to make. Getting ahead is an essential element for me, so I'll make all the components for this 2 days before so the delectable flavours infuse, and then it's just a matter of spooning into small jars when I want to serve them.

FOR THE TOMATO DIP

2 TBSP OLIVE OIL

200G CHERRY TOMATOES

2 GARLIC CLOVES, CRUSHED

1/2 SMALL LEMON, JUICE ONLY

1 TSP SUGAR

SALT AND FRESHLY GROUND BLACK PEPPER

FOR THE PESTO

50G HAZELNUTS, TOASTED

2 GARLIC CLOVES, ROUGHLY CHOPPED

1/2 LEMON, ZEST AND JUICE

1/2 RED CHILLI, CHOPPED

150ML EXTRA VIRGIN OLIVE OIL

50G GRATED PARMESAN

SALT AND FRESHLY GROUND BLACK PEPPER, TO TASTE

FOR THE CIABATTA

3 TBSP RAPESEED OIL

1 TBSP CHOPPED PARSLEY

12 VERY THIN SLICES CIABATTA, FLATTENED WITH A ROLLING PIN

SEA SALT

100G GREEK-STYLE NATURAL YOGHURT

To make the tomato dip, heat the olive oil in a medium saucepan, add the cherry tomatoes and sauté for 2 to 3 minutes until they just burst. Add the garlic, lemon juice and sugar and sauté for a further 3 minutes. Season with salt and freshly ground black pepper. Crush the tomatoes lightly and set aside to cool completely.

To make the pesto, place the hazelnuts, garlic, lemon zest and juice, red chilli and 4 tbsp of extra virgin olive oil in a food processor and pulse a few times until roughly chopped. While the motor is still running, slowly pour in the remaining extra virgin olive oil. Add the Parmesan. Check the seasoning, adding a little salt if needed and freshly ground black pepper.

To prepare the ciabatta, preheat the oven to 220°C/fan 200°C/gas 7. Combine the rapeseed oil and chopped parsley and brush onto both sides of the flattened ciabatta. Toast for about 5 minutes, but keep an eye on them as they tend to burn. Sprinkle a little sea salt on one side of each piece.

To assemble, spoon 3 tbsp of the cold tomato dip, 3 tbsp of natural yoghurt and 2 tbsp of pesto into each glass jar. Place on a board or platter and serve with the ciabatta.

FARMHOUSE SOUPS

My Favourite Soups

Bowlfuls of nostalgia! That's what soups are to me. They were, and still are, staples for us on the farm, comforting in the winter and filling in the summer. Mastering the art of soup making is easy: it's all about building layers of flavour by adding meats, such as beef, ham, chicken, pancetta and chorizo, or spices, such as cumin, ginger, coriander or curry powder, or handfuls of herbs. Even blue cheese works well in some soups. We bulk soups with egg noodles or rice but my favourite is a more traditional one – a root vegetable soup thickened with potato. Soups are one of life's little comforts. When everything around gets hectic, I like nothing more than retreating to the armchair, cradling a mug of soup and enjoying every sip – after which I always feel much better and ready to tackle the world again!

How to …
Make great Vegetable and Chicken Stock

Stock is one of the fundamental basics in the kitchen here at Ballyknocken, and a good stock is the secret to a great soup. Here are some of our cookery school tips on how to make the best base for your soups.

❖❖❖

Vegetable stock

You'll need about 500g of chopped carrots, chopped celery sticks and leaves, chopped fennel, roughly chopped onions, shallots or leeks and/or their trimmings (carrot peelings etc. are just fine, but not onion or shallot skins, which will discolour the stock), a bunch of parsley (it doesn't matter if it is wilted), 2 large sprigs of thyme (and other herbs of your choice) and 10 whole black peppercorns. Heat a little rapeseed oil in a stock pot or large saucepan, add the vegetables and/or trimmings and sauté for about 10 minutes, stirring from time to time, before adding 2 litres of cold water. Bring to the boil, then reduce the heat and simmer gently for about 30 minutes. Pass the stock through a sieve. Cool and then freeze in portions in ziplock bags so it's easy to add to soups, casseroles and sauces.

❖❖❖

Chicken stock

You'll need the carcass from Sunday's roast chicken, 250g trimmed, roughly chopped vegetables, a handful of parsley and 2 cloves of garlic. Heat a little rapeseed oil in a stock pot or large saucepan, add the carcass, vegetables, parsley and garlic and sauté for about 10 minutes. Pour in 2 litres of cold water and bring to the boil. Reduce the heat and simmer for 3 hours. Pass the stock through a sieve and leave to cool. The fat will rise to the top and harden when cold, making it easy to remove and discard. Then freeze in portions as for vegetable stock above.

DUO OF SOUPS
BEETROOT AND JERUSALEM ARTICHOKE WITH BACON

Serves 4

Both of these vegetables are no-fuss and easy to grow, which is my type of veg! In fact, the Jerusalem artichokes keep producing year on year – I don't have to interfere at all. They are a bit fiddly to peel but so worth it. Their flavour is quite earthy, so I like to add some depth with smoked bacon or chorizo, or sun-dried tomatoes for a vegetarian option.

FOR THE BEETROOT SOUP

EXTRA VIRGIN OLIVE OIL, FOR SAUTÉING

1 ONION, FINELY CHOPPED

1 MEDIUM CARROT, DICED

1 TSP CHOPPED THYME

1 LITRE VEGETABLE STOCK

4 COOKED BEETROOT, CHOPPED

2 TSP CHOPPED DILL

SALT AND FRESHLY GROUND BLACK PEPPER

FOR THE JERUSALEM ARTICHOKE SOUP

EXTRA VIRGIN OLIVE OIL, FOR SAUTÉING

50G SMOKED BACON LARDONS

1 ONION, FINELY CHOPPED

2 GARLIC CLOVES, CHOPPED

1 TBSP CHOPPED CHIVES

20 MEDIUM JERUSALEM ARTICHOKES, PEELED AND DICED

1 LITRE VEGETABLE STOCK

50ML CREAM

SALT AND FRESHLY GROUND BLACK PEPPER

2 TSP CHOPPED CHIVES, TO GARNISH

To make the beetroot soup, heat the oil in a large saucepan, add the onion and carrot and sauté for about 6 minutes until just soft. Stir in the thyme, pour in the vegetable stock and add the beetroot. Simmer for about 20 minutes, until the carrot has softened. Stir in the dill, then check the seasoning, adding salt and freshly ground black pepper as necessary. Ladle the soup into a blender and purée until smooth. Return to the saucepan and add extra vegetable stock if too thick.

To make the Jerusalem artichoke soup, heat a little oil in a large saucepan over a medium heat.

Add the lardons and sauté until crispy. Remove with a slotted spoon and drain on kitchen paper.

Add the onion and sauté until softened but not browned. Add the garlic and cook for 2 minutes.

Stir in the chives, Jerusalem artichokes and vegetable stock and simmer for about 20 minutes, until the artichokes are soft. Return the crispy smoked bacon to the soup. Add the cream and simmer for about 2 minutes. Check the seasoning, adding salt and freshly ground black pepper to taste. Ladle the soup into a food processor and blend until smooth. Check the seasoning again and return to the saucepan – add some extra vegetable stock if too thick.

To serve, heat the soups, then pour each into a separate large jug. Pour both soups at the same time into warm soup bowls. Using a fork, gently swirl the soups together.

Sprinkle the chives into the centre of each bowl and serve immediately.

Sorrel, Wild Garlic and Potato Soup

Serves 4

We grow French sorrel, which is truly delicious in sauces and soups. It has a slight lemony bite to it, making it perfect with the wild garlic in this recipe.

2 TBSP RAPESEED OIL

2 MEDIUM ONIONS, FINELY DICED

SMALL BUNDLE WILD GARLIC, CHOPPED

1 TBSP CHOPPED PARSLEY

3 MEDIUM POTATOES, DICED

1.2 LITRES VEGETABLE STOCK

100G FRENCH SORREL, TRIMMED AND ROUGHLY CHOPPED, PLUS EXTRA TO GARNISH

100ML CREAM

SALT AND FRESHLY GROUND BLACK PEPPER

Heat the oil in a large saucepan, add the onions and sauté for 6 to 7 minutes until softened but not browned. Add the wild garlic and cook for a further 2 minutes, then stir in the parsley and potatoes.

Add the stock and simmer for 15 to 20 minutes. Stir in the sorrel and simmer for about 2 minutes.

Add to a blender and purée until smooth. Return to the saucepan and then add the cream – and some more stock if too thick. Reheat gently. Check the seasoning, adding salt and freshly ground black pepper as required.

To serve, ladle into warm soup bowls and garnish with chopped sorrel.

CURRIED MUSSEL SOUP

Serves 4

This is an elegant dinner-party-style soup – it's quite filling, though, so it's good to opt for a lighter main course to follow. We have an abundance of wonderful mussels here in Ireland, so we should use them more in home cooking. They take flavour very well and are particularly tasty with curry spices.

FOR THE BROTH

1KG FRESH MUSSELS

2 TBSP BUTTER

1 MEDIUM ONION, FINELY DICED

2 GARLIC CLOVES, CRUSHED

1 MEDIUM RED CHILLI, DESEEDED AND FINELY DICED

1/2 FENNEL BULB, FINELY SLICED

100ML DRY WHITE WINE

400ML VEGETABLE STOCK

FOR THE SOUP

3 TBSP BUTTER

4 TBSP FLOUR

1 TSP MADRAS CURRY POWDER

400ML VEGETABLE STOCK

4 TBSP SHERRY

200ML DOUBLE CREAM

SALT AND FRESHLY GROUND BLACK PEPPER

FOR THE TOPPING

1 MEDIUM CARROT, PEELED AND FINELY DICED

1/2 FENNEL BULB, FINELY DICED

1/2 CELERY STICK, FINELY DICED

2 TSP CHOPPED PARSLEY

4 TBSP SOUR CREAM, TO GARNISH

To make the broth, first clean the mussels by scrubbing or scraping the shells under cold running water to remove seaweed, barnacles and mud. Pull away any 'beards' hanging from the mussels. Then drain them and discard any that are cracked or have opened.

Melt the butter in a large saucepan over a medium to high heat. Add the onion, garlic and chilli and sauté for 4 to 5 minutes. Add the fennel and simmer for a further 2 minutes. Pour in the white wine and bring to the boil. Stir in the vegetable stock and bring to the boil again before adding the mussels.

Cover with a tight-fitting lid and cook for 2 to 3 minutes, shaking the saucepan occasionally, until the mussels are open. Strain the mussels, keeping the broth. Scoop the mussels out of their shells and place in a bowl. Discard any that remain closed.

To make the soup, put the butter, flour and curry powder into a large saucepan over a medium heat and stir well before adding the vegetable stock and the mussel broth. Keep stirring until it thickens slightly. Add the sherry and cream and stir well. Return the mussels to the saucepan and heat through. Check the seasoning, adding salt and a little freshly ground black pepper to taste.

To prepare the topping, combine all the ingredients.

To serve, ladle the soup into warm bowls. Top with the finely chopped vegetables and garnish with a little sour cream.

SHALLOT, SPINACH AND BARLEY SOUP

Serves 4

I'm delighted to see that barley has had a resurgence in the kitchen. It's delicious for risotto and especially tasty in this soup. It adds good texture and a slightly nutty flavour to dishes.

2 TBSP EXTRA VIRGIN OLIVE OIL

5 SHALLOTS, FINELY SLICED

1 GARLIC CLOVE, THINLY SLICED

½ TSP CUMIN

1 POTATO, DICED

2 CELERY STICKS, SLICED ON THE DIAGONAL

50G BARLEY

1.2 LITRES VEGETABLE STOCK

100G SPINACH, TRIMMED AND ROUGHLY CHOPPED

SALT AND FRESHLY GROUND BLACK PEPPER

2 TBSP CRÈME FRAÎCHE, TO GARNISH

A FEW CELERY SPRIGS, TO GARNISH

Heat the olive oil in a large saucepan. Add the shallots and sauté for 4 to 5 minutes until softened but not browned. Add the garlic and cumin and cook for a further 2 minutes, then stir in the diced potato, celery and barley. Pour in the stock and simmer for 15 to 20 minutes until the vegetables are soft. Stir in the spinach and simmer for a further 1 minute until the spinach has just wilted. Check the seasoning, adding salt and freshly ground black pepper as required.

To serve, ladle into warm soup bowls, spoon some crème fraîche in the centre of each and place a celery sprig in the middle.

Kale, Cannellini and Potato Soup

Serves 4

This is where Italy meets Ireland – yes, it's my taste nod to Italy and a really delicious and healthy blend of our two cultures.

OLIVE OIL, FOR SAUTÉING

1 LARGE ONION, THINLY SLICED

2 GARLIC CLOVES, THINLY SLICED

60G SMOKED BACON, DICED

4 MEDIUM POTATOES, PEELED AND DICED

1 TSP CHOPPED THYME

100ML WHITE WINE

1.2 LITRES VEGETABLE STOCK

SALT AND FRESHLY GROUND BLACK PEPPER

60G CURLY KALE, WASHED AND ROUGHLY SHREDDED

150G COOKED CANNELLINI BEANS

Heat a little olive oil in a large saucepan and sauté the onion for 5 minutes until soft and just starting to colour. Add the garlic and cook for 1 minute. Add the smoked bacon and sauté until fairly crispy. Add the potatoes, thyme and white wine and sauté for 3 minutes, stirring from time to time.

Pour in the vegetable stock, bring to the boil, then reduce the heat. Check the seasoning, adding salt and freshly ground black pepper to taste. Simmer for about 18 to 20 minutes.

Stir in the kale and cooked beans and simmer for about 3 to 4 minutes, until the kale is just tender.

Ladle into soup bowls and serve.

FRESH CATCH

Fish Mains

Walking along the Murrough near Wicklow Town, I'm always in awe of the dedicated sea anglers, who patiently wait in varying weather for their catch to bite. There's good fishing in the Irish Sea between Greystones and Wicklow Town, with bass, mackerel, mullet, sea trout, wrasse and pollack popular with anglers. And we have well stocked rivers too – I'm especially partial to Avonmore River trout. Despite this abundance, we Irish often seem to be nervous about cooking fish at home, so I hope the fish recipes in this chapter will encourage more people to give it a go!

How to …
Cook fish

Through teaching our ever-popular Mastering Fish and Sauces cookery class, I have heard many students say that, whilst they love fish, they tend to only order it in restaurants. This is partly because it's often overcooked at home, just to be sure! Learning how not to overcook fish is important, as it cooks surprisingly quickly. When correctly cooked, it flakes away very gently and is ever so slightly transparent and juicy. As a general rule, whatever method you use, for every 2.5 cm (1 inch) height of fish allow 10 minutes for it to cook.

❈

Pan-frying
fish fillets

First dust your fish fillets with a little flour, then preheat a large non-stick frying pan with 1 tbsp rapeseed oil over a medium heat. Now add a small amount of butter and allow this to foam. If the fish has skin on, score the skin, which helps to prevent it curling up. Then place the fillet in the pan, skin side down first, and fry for about 2 to 2½ minutes depending on the thickness of the fillet. Use a fish slice to carefully press it down. Turn over and cook for 1 to 2 minutes on the other side. Always brush the oil generously onto the fish and not the pan.

❈

Roasting
whole fish or fillets

Preheat the oven to 180°C/fan 160°C/gas 4. Then stuff the cavity of a whole fish with dill and slices of lemon and fennel – often I'll place it on a bed of vegetables like leeks, shallots and peppers. Drizzle with rapeseed oil, sprinkle over some sea salt and freshly ground black pepper or spoon over herb oil. Roasting a whole fish generally takes between 18 and 22 minutes, but this does depend on the size and thickness. If you have small individual fillets, it's a good idea to place them one on top of the other (head to toe, so to speak), with a layer of sharp pesto spread between them. Then tie with string, pop into a roasting tin, spoon over a little oil and season with salt and some freshly ground black pepper. These will take about 15 to 18 minutes to roast, depending on the size.

GRILLING
Whole fish, fillets or steaks

Because of the intense direct heat, grilling can be a little tricky depending on the thickness of the fish. I tend to set my oven to a medium temperature and on the oven/grill setting. This way, my fish colours nicely on top whilst cooking fully through. I also line my grill with buttered foil to catch the juices, and I baste the fish with melted butter or a flavoured oil, such as chilli oil, while grilling.

TO GRILL WHOLE FISH Add your flavours – such as lime, lemon, dill, leeks, shallots and onion – to the cavity. Then brush the fish with oil and place a few small pieces of flavoured butter on top. Baste once or twice while cooking and turn the fish over. It's difficult to give accurate timings, as every grill differs in heat intensity, but as a general rule, the timing is usually 10 minutes for 2.5 cm thickness and 20 minutes for 5cm thickness under a medium-hot grill. **TO GRILL FISH FILLETS OR STEAKS** Baste generously with melted butter, season with salt and pepper and maybe some lemon zest. Turn over halfway through to ensure the fish is fully cooked.

HOT SMOKING
Salmon

Salmon is quite easy to smoke at home. It's a two-part process: first the salmon needs to be cured, which can take anything from 3 to 24 hours, depending on the size of the fish fillet; then it's hot smoked.

We use this dry rub for curing salmon in the cookery school: light brown sugar and salt (the brown sugar gives a beautiful colour). Then we adjust the flavours by adding our choice of the following: orange and lemon zest, fennel seeds, pink peppercorns, dill and fennel herb or any other herbs.

For a quick cure and hot smoke use the tail ends of salmon, as they are thinner and therefore quicker to process. Cover them in the dry rub then place in a flat dish and seal it with clingfilm. Leave in the fridge for 3 to 4 hours then rub off the sugar-salt mix and pat the fish dry.

When curing a whole side of salmon, the tail and underbelly portions, being thin, will absorb more salt than the rest, so I would recommend slicing them off and adding them later, or using a thinner layer of the curing mix on them. The thick parts will need 6 to 8 hours of curing in the fridge, before rubbing off and patting dry.

For hot smoking, the wood chips need to be dried and seasoned, free of any varnish, wood preservatives or contaminants. Fresh-cut wood with its natural sap will leave a very bad, bitter taste on food. Salmon can take quite a strong smoke flavour so I would recommend alder for an elegant, rounded flavour, birch or ash for a delicate flavour or oak for an intense, bold flavour. If you can't find any of the above woods, maple, cherry, apple or pear will do – these add a slightly sweet flavour to foods. (The hickory, mesquite, Jack Daniels oak-barrel or even Jameson oak-barrel chippings that are widely available for smoking are really good for pork ribs but are a little strong for delicate fish.)

First you need to soak the wood chips. Soaking them in bulk for about a day and then placing into several bags and freezing them is a great way to have barbecue-ready wood chips any time of the year. Otherwise, just soak two handfuls for about 4 hours before smoking.

Prepare your wood or charcoal barbecue as usual and when it is ready spread the wood chips on top of the hot coals, place the fish on the grill, cover with the lid and barbecue as normal. The tails will only take about 4–5 minutes skin side down. Serve immediately. If you plan to serve cold, you can very slightly undercook the salmon, as it will continue to cook while cooling down.

Tomato Haddock with Asparagus and Prosciutto

Serves 4

This is one of the most popular fish dishes that we make in our cookery school, yet it's easy and can be done in a flash.

FOR THE TOMATO BASE

RAPESEED OIL

3 GARLIC CLOVES, FINELY CHOPPED

200ML PASSATA

1/2 ORANGE, ZEST ONLY

2 TSP OREGANO, CHOPPED

1/2 TSP CELERY SEEDS

SALT AND FRESHLY GROUND BLACK PEPPER

FOR THE ROAST TOMATOES

250G CHERRY TOMATOES ON THE VINE

1 TSP CHOPPED ROSEMARY

1 TBSP CHOPPED CHIVES

12 ASPARAGUS SPEARS, TRIMMED

FOR THE FISH

4 X 170G HADDOCK OR COD FILLETS

100G PROSCIUTTO DI PARMA

SPRIGS OF ROSEMARY, TO SERVE

Heat the oven to 190°C/fan 170°C/gas 5.

To make the tomato base, heat a little oil in a shallow casserole dish on the hob, add the garlic and cook for 1 minute. Pour in the passata, orange zest, oregano and celery seeds and simmer slowly for 10 minutes. Season with salt and freshly ground black pepper.

For the roast tomatoes, place the tomatoes on the vine on top of the sauce, drizzle over a little rapeseed oil, add the rosemary and chives and roast in the oven for about 10 minutes.

Meanwhile, add the asparagus to rapidly boiling water and cook for 2 minutes. Drain and then place in ice-cold water.

For the fish, place 3 spears of the blanched asparagus on each fillet and wrap with prosciutto di Parma. Place in the casserole dish around the cherry tomatoes and return to the oven for about 10 to 12 minutes until the fish is just cooked through.

Serve with Garlic and Rosemary Roast Potatoes (see p. 136) and garnish with sprigs of rosemary.

Baked Trout with Fennel, Lime and Wasabi Cream Sauce

Serves 4

For this recipe the trout are baked whole. Sea bream and mackerel also work very well baked as whole fish with zingy lengths of spring onions, lime and plenty of dill stuffed in the cavity and served with lightly toasted hazelnuts, lemon zest and chervil sprinkled over the top.

SUNFLOWER OIL, FOR OILING AND DRIZZLING

4 RAINBOW TROUT, GUTTED AND CLEANED

1 FENNEL BULB, FINELY SLICED

1 LIME, SLICED IN 8

PARSLEY, THYME AND DILL SPRIGS

SALT AND FRESHLY GROUND BLACK PEPPER

FOR THE SAUCE

1 TBSP BUTTER

3 SHALLOTS, FINELY CHOPPED

1 GARLIC CLOVE, VERY FINELY CHOPPED

1 LIME, ZEST AND JUICE

100ML DOUBLE CREAM

1 TBSP CHOPPED CHIVES

1/4 TSP WASABI PASTE

12 ASPARAGUS SPEARS, TRIMMED AND BLANCHED

SUNFLOWER OIL, FOR BRUSHING

2 TBSP TOASTED FLAKED ALMONDS, TO GARNISH

4 TO 5 SPRIGS OF DILL, TO GARNISH

Preheat the oven to 200°C/fan 180°C/gas 6.

Place the trout on an oiled roasting tray. Open the cavity and drizzle with a little oil. Place some slices of fennel in the cavity of each trout and arrange 3 slices of lime on top. Sprinkle the herbs over the fish and drizzle with oil. Season with salt and freshly ground black pepper and roast for about 20 minutes until the flesh is soft to touch.

To make the sauce, heat the butter in a saucepan over a medium heat. Add the shallots and sauté for about 3 minutes. Stir in the garlic and cook for a further 1 minute. Add the lime zest and juice, cream, chives and wasabi. Stir well until it thickens slightly.

Heat a chargrill pan over a medium heat, brush the asparagus spears with a little oil and chargrill on both sides. Transfer to a platter and keep warm.

To serve, lift the fish onto the asparagus, sprinkle over the flaked almonds and spoon over some sauce. Garnish with sprigs of dill.

Smoked Salmon and Salmon Fish Cakes

Makes 12

These are my surprise fish cakes – smoked salmon in salmon! So if you can't make your mind up which one you prefer, go for both and make this recipe.

FOR THE FISH CAKES

300G SALMON, POACHED AND FLAKED

200G MASHED POTATOES

3 SPRING ONIONS, VERY FINELY CHOPPED

1 TBSP CHOPPED CHIVES

3 TBSP CAPERS, DRAINED AND CHOPPED

SALT AND FRESHLY GROUND BLACK PEPPER

100G SMOKED SALMON, FINELY CHOPPED

1 LARGE FREE-RANGE EGG, BEATEN

50G BROWN BREADCRUMBS

1 TBSP FINELY CHOPPED PARSLEY

BUTTER AND OIL, FOR FRYING

FOR THE SAUCE

1 TBSP CHOPPED CHIVES

LARGE BUNCH OF FLAT-LEAF PARSLEY, FINELY CHOPPED

½ LEMON, JUICE AND ZEST

4 SUNDRIED TOMATO HALVES, FINELY CHOPPED

2 TBSP TOASTED PINE NUTS, FINELY CHOPPED

100ML EXTRA VIRGIN OLIVE OIL

WATERCRESS OR SALAD LEAVES, TO GARNISH

BORAGE FLOWERS, TO GARNISH

LEMON WEDGES, TO SERVE

To make the fish cakes, place the flaked salmon, mashed potatoes, spring onions, chives and capers in a bowl. Season with salt and freshly ground black pepper. Divide the mixture into 12 portions and, using damp hands, place about a tablespoon of chopped smoked salmon in the centre of the salmon and potato mix and shape into medium-sized fish cakes.

Pour the beaten egg into a shallow bowl. Mix the breadcrumbs and parsley together and transfer to a plate. Dip each fish cake in the egg and then roll in the parsley breadcrumbs. Place on a plate lined with parchment paper and set aside in the fridge for about 20 minutes.

Heat some butter and oil in a frying pan over a medium heat and carefully fry the cakes for about 2 to 3 minutes on each side until lightly golden brown.

To make the sauce, whisk all the ingredients in a small bowl and set aside.

To serve, place 3 cakes on each serving plate, spoon over the sauce and serve with salad leaves, borage flowers and lemon wedges.

Walking along the Murragh near Wicklow Town, I'm always in awe of the dedicated sea anglers, who patiently wait in varying weather for their catch to bite.

Baked Oysters with Bacon

Makes 24

This is a very traditional recipe, a favourite of my mother's and found in many older cookbooks. While we were filming the TV series *Lords and Ladles*, we created a version of these at the beautiful Ballywalter Park, home of the most gracious of hosts, Lord and Lady Dunleath.

24 SHUCKED OYSTERS

12 RASHERS GOOD QUALITY BACON OR PANCETTA, SLICED IN HALF

24 COCKTAIL STICKS

LARGE KNOB OF BUTTER

4 TBSP BREADCRUMBS

1 TBSP FINELY CHOPPED PARSLEY

GENEROUS HANDFUL SEAWEED, TO GARNISH

OYSTER SHELLS, FOR PRESENTATION

HANDFUL ROCKET LEAVES

Preheat the grill on high.

Wrap each oyster in a bacon rasher and secure with a cocktail stick. Place on an oiled baking tray under the grill until the bacon is crispy. Keep an eye on them.

For the topping, heat the butter in a frying pan over a medium heat. Add the breadcrumbs and lightly brown. Remove from the heat and add the chopped parsley. Mix well and set aside.

Bring a saucepan of water to the boil and drop in the seaweed for just a few seconds. As soon as it becomes a brighter green, transfer the seaweed to iced water, then drain. Place in a layer on the serving platter with the oyster shells on top.

Put a few rocket leaves into each oyster shell. Take the cocktail sticks out of the wrapped oysters and arrange the oysters in the shells.

To serve, spoon some breadcrumbs over each oyster and serve immediately.

The Murrough Posh Fish Pie

Serves 4

This was my mother's signature fish dish. We traipsed around the whole island of Ireland with this dish as she entered fish-cookery competitions across the country. She used to present the pie in scallop shells and as kids we used to think, 'How posh!' Now I think, 'How very 1980s!'

MELTED BUTTER, FOR BRUSHING

FOR THE FILLING

300ML MILK

2 BAY LEAVES

3 TBSP BUTTER

4 TBSP PLAIN FLOUR

SALT AND FRESHLY GROUND BLACK PEPPER

2 TSP CHOPPED PARSLEY

2 TSP ROUGHLY CHOPPED CHERVIL

150G SMOKED HADDOCK, DICED

150G SALMON, DICED

200G SKINLESS WHITE FISH SUCH AS HADDOCK, COD OR POLLACK, DICED

150G PRAWNS, SHELLED

FOR THE MASHED POTATOES

4 LARGE POTATOES, STEAMED

30G BUTTER

100ML MILK

PINCH OF NUTMEG

SALT AND FRESHLY GROUND BLACK PEPPER

FOR THE MASHED SWEET POTATO

1 MEDIUM SWEET POTATO, STEAMED

2 TO 3 TBSP MILK

1 TBSP BUTTER

SALT AND FRESHLY GROUND BLACK PEPPER

Brush a medium-sized gratin dish with melted butter. Preheat the oven to 180°C/fan 160°C/gas 4.

To prepare the filling, pour the milk into a medium saucepan over a medium heat with the bay leaves, butter and flour and stir until a thick sauce forms. Season with salt and freshly ground black pepper and add the chopped parsley and chervil. Add the diced fish and prawns to the sauce and simmer gently until the fish is just cooked. This should take about 5 minutes. Check the seasoning again.

To prepare the potatoes, push the warm potatoes through a ricer. Warm the milk and butter in the microwave and add to the potatoes with a little grated nutmeg, salt and pepper. Spoon into a piping bag with a star nozzle.

Now mash the sweet potatoes and add the milk, butter, salt and pepper. Spoon into another piping bag with another star nozzle.

To assemble, spoon the fish into the gratin dish. Pipe a line of sweet potato diagonally across and then pipe the potato over the rest of the pie.

Place in the oven for about 12 to 15 minutes until the top is lightly golden. Serve with a green salad.

IRISH SEAFOOD RISOTTO

Serves 4

I'm partial to a good risotto. Rice takes flavours so well, especially seafood. This is a recipe you can experiment with, changing the fish to your taste. I particularly like octopus and clams in mine.

EXTRA VIRGIN OLIVE OIL, FOR SAUTÉING

100G PANCETTA, SLICED INTO LARDONS

KNOB OF BUTTER

6 SHALLOTS, FINELY SLICED

1 LEEK, SLICED

1 GARLIC CLOVE, CHOPPED

400G RISOTTO RICE

150ML WHITE WINE

1.5 LITRES LIGHT FISH STOCK, HEATED TO SIMMERING

250G MONKFISH, DICED

100G PRAWNS, SHELLED

2 SQUID TUBES, SLICED AND PRESOAKED IN MILK TO TENDERISE, THEN RINSED WELL

1 TSP CHOPPED TARRAGON

1/2 LEMON, ZEST AND JUICE

1 TBSP CHOPPED PARSLEY

200G STEAMED MUSSELS

SALT AND FRESHLY GROUND BLACK PEPPER

SPRIGS OF TARRAGON, TO GARNISH

LEMON WEDGES, TO SERVE

Heat a little oil in a large heavy saucepan over a medium to high heat. Add the pancetta lardons and sauté until crispy. Transfer to a piece of kitchen paper to drain.

Add 2 tbsp oil and the butter to the saucepan. When the butter is foaming, add the shallots and leek and cook for 5 minutes until beginning to soften. Add the garlic and rice, and cook for a few minutes until the rice is shiny and opaque. Add the wine and bring to the boil for 1 minute, stirring constantly.

Reduce the heat and add the stock, a ladleful at a time, stirring constantly until each ladleful is absorbed. Add the monkfish, prawns, squid and tarragon before the last ladle. Simmer for 2 to 3 minutes until the fish is cooked.

Return the pancetta to the saucepan. Add the lemon zest and juice, parsley and steamed mussels. Stir carefully and heat through. Check the seasoning, adding salt and freshly ground black pepper to taste.

Serve in warm bowls and garnish with sprigs of tarragon and lemon wedges.

OF PASTURES FAIR

Meaty Mains

As I look across the fields, I'm constantly reminded of how beautiful this county is. I can't help it – I'm a very proud Wicklow woman! The pastures and hillsides of Wicklow offer amazing vegetation for our sheep to forage on. They are out and about in the fresh air, keeping themselves fit by grazing up and down the hills. You can't ask for a better formula for producing good flavoured Wicklow lamb and for that reason I'm very partial to it. Even though we sometimes complain about the weather, we are very lucky to have this mix of rain and sunshine, which results in fantastic grass growth. That, coupled with the mild winters, means that cattle can enjoy the pastures for longer, resulting in high quality and flavoursome meat. Living so close to the Wicklow Mountains, we are also fortunate to enjoy some delicious wild game – the venison and pheasant being particularly tasty.

How to ...
COOK MEAT

The trick to cooking meat is the caramelisation – that's when the meat juices sweeten and crisp up to bring an irreplaceable flavour to a dish. We spend lots of time discussing and debating the best ways to cook meat with our guests in our cookery school, so here are some of our tips, the first of which is to use a meat thermometer for the best results when cooking meat. You can refer to the guidelines in the table below.

CHICKEN	PORK	LAMB & BEEF		
80°C	75°C	55°C	65°C	75°C
Must be cooked through	Must be cooked through	Rare	Medium	Well done

Roasting

This is one of the easiest ways to cook large cuts of meat such as lamb shoulder, pork fillet, loin of pork, shoulder of pork, rolled rib of beef, brisket or top rib/housekeeper's cut – and once the meat is in the oven, you can relax! Using a rub or marinade on the meat will give you extra flavour. Always preheat the oven, then start off the cooking process at about 190°C/fan 170°C/gas 5 for the first 30 minutes to brown the meat, and then reduce to 180°C/fan 160°C/gas 4. Keep basting throughout to ensure a moist roast. Placing a trivet of roughly chopped vegetables under the meat will give good flavour to both the meat and gravy and allow heat to circulate evenly around the meat.

No V 28800 DUN LAOGHAIRE

the Royal Bank of Ireland

address on their visit
cheerful Red Red on the
place & the Subscription
expires next year he wishes
you to obtain a Stay
of prosecution if possible

DANIEL CONNER
FLOWER MAIN STREET

Mrs O'Connor & Co

ng, the Plaintiff may
in your absence.
day of November in the
hundred and one

Form F.

Irish Land

ESTATES COMMISSI

Copy
Agreement between Vendor
Tenant for Sale of a Holding.

Record No. E.C. 3783

COUNTY Wicklow

ESTATE OF
R. J. Welch & others

TENANT Patrick Byrne

Samuel Kerr

YEATES, Law Stationers, Stamp
& Newsagents, 74 Dame St.

66 Dame Street
Dublin
Solicitor

Chargrilling

This is a perfect way to cook mini chicken fillets, lamb steaks, lamb cutlets and chops, beef fillets, sirloin, T-bone and rump steaks. First ensure that your chargrill pan is non-stick. Second ensure that the meat, not the chargrill pan, is brushed with oil. It's best to begin with a medium to high heat. Let the meat seal before you try to turn it over. A dry rub of mixed herbs, spices, salt and pepper is best for seasoning when chargrilling. (See p. 104 for sample dry rub recipe).

Stir-frying

Probably one of my favourite methods and also the fastest – I stir-fry a lot during the week. Ensure the strips of meat you're going to use are thinly cut and marinate them first for flavour and tenderness. The wok must be hot before you add the oil – then keep it at a constant high heat and move the meat around the sides of the wok.

Frying

I find that this method can splatter and be messy so I made a great investment by purchasing a simple splatter guard. Every home should have one! The cuts to use are similar to those for chargrilling: chicken fillets, lamb steaks, cutlets and chops, beef fillets, sirloin, T-bone and rump steaks. Season the meat before placing in the hot pan and don't turn it over until it has browned/caramelised underneath.

Poaching

Poaching has great health benefits. It's also quick and keeps meats like chicken moist and flavoursome. Chicken fillets poach incredibly well in a spicy broth for soup – just add noodles. An easy poaching liquid is ✿ white wine, ✿ vegetable stock and ✿ water; add 1 tbsp chopped parsley, 2 tsp chopped thyme and 2 bay leaves – this gives a good base of flavours.

Herby Parmesan-Encrusted Rack of Wicklow Lamb with Plum Salsa

Serves 4

This one's a dinner-party special – the sweetness of the plums connects with the herby, salty Parmesan crust and blends beautifully with our wonderful Wicklow lamb.

FOR THE LAMB

2 TBSP HONEY

1 TBSP BALSAMIC VINEGAR

1 TBSP EXTRA VIRGIN OLIVE OIL, PLUS EXTRA FOR BRUSHING

2 X 4 CUTLET RACKS OF LAMB (2 CUTLETS PER PERSON)

FOR THE HERB CRUST

2 TSP FINELY CHOPPED THYME

¼ TSP DRIED RED CHILLI

½ TSP SALT

3 TBSP GRATED PARMESAN

1 TSP WHOLEGRAIN MUSTARD

4 TBSP BREADCRUMBS

1 TBSP EXTRA VIRGIN OLIVE OIL

3 LARGE MINT LEAVES, FINELY CHOPPED

SALT AND FRESHLY GROUND BLACK PEPPER

FOR THE SALSA

3 PLUMS, DICED

8 BLACKBERRIES

1 TSP SUGAR

4 LARGE MINT LEAVES, FINELY CHOPPED

4 TBSP EXTRA VIRGIN OLIVE OIL

½ LEMON, JUICE ONLY

Preheat the oven to 180°C/fan 160°C/gas 4.

To prepare the lamb, place the honey, balsamic vinegar and oil in a small bowl, mix well and spread over the meat.

Mix all the ingredients for the crust in a bowl and stir well.

Brush the racks of lamb with some oil. Spread or pat the crust mixture onto the racks of lamb.

Place the lamb in a large roasting tin and put in the oven for about 30 to 35 minutes, depending on how well done you like it. Take it out of the oven, cover loosely and allow to rest for 10 minutes.

To make the salsa, put all the ingredients into a small bowl and mix well.

To serve, slice each rack into chops and serve with Mustard and Spinach Mash (see p. 135) and the plum salsa.

Leg of Wicklow Lamb with Moroccan Mint Jelly and Shallot and Red Wine Gravy

Serves 6 to 8

We have Moroccan mint in a pot near the school so – perhaps through sheer laziness on my part, as it's nearest the door – it gets used a lot! I use it as a tea as well and it makes a really good cordial during the summer.

FOR THE MINT JELLY

you will need to make this a day ahead

400G APPLES, SKIN ON, DICED

1 CUP FRESH MOROCCAN MINT LEAVES

50ML LEMON JUICE

600ML WATER

JAM SUGAR, AS REQUIRED

FOR THE LEG OF LAMB

1 TSP GROUND CUMIN

1 TSP FINELY CHOPPED ROSEMARY

1 LEMON, ZEST ONLY

1 TBSP HONEY

3 TBSP OLIVE OIL, PLUS EXTRA FOR DRIZZLING

1.5KG LEG OF LAMB, TRIMMED

5 MEDIUM GARLIC CLOVES, SLICED IN HALF LENGTHWAYS

To make the jelly, first put a saucer in the freezer. Next place the apples, mint, lemon juice and water into a large saucepan and simmer for 30 minutes until the apples are soft. Sieve through a cloth into a large bowl, letting it drip through slowly. Measure the juice collected. For every 250ml apple-mint liquid you will need 185g of jam sugar. Place the juice and appropriate amount of jam sugar in a saucepan and simmer for about 30 minutes.

To test, take the saucer out of the freezer. Spoon a little jelly onto it and place in the fridge. Leave for a few minutes, then pull your finger through the centre. If the jelly wrinkles and remains separated, then it is ready. If it doesn't, put the saucepan back on the heat, simmer for a further 5 minutes and then re-test.

For the lamb, mix the cumin, rosemary, lemon zest, honey and oil in a small bowl. Spread this over the meat and leave for 30 minutes. (Always allow the lamb to come to room temperature before roasting – this will take about 30 minutes.)

Meanwhile, preheat the oven to 200°C/fan 180°C/ gas 6.

10 SMALL SPRIGS OF
ROSEMARY

SALT AND FRESHLY GROUND
BLACK PEPPER

FOR THE GRAVY

6 SHALLOTS, SLICED

2 GARLIC CLOVES, CRUSHED

200ML RED WINE

1 TBSP TOMATO PURÉE

1 TSP HONEY

400ML LAMB OR VEGETABLE
STOCK

2 TSP CORNFLOUR MIXED
WITH 2 TBSP COLD STOCK
OR WATER

SALT AND FRESHLY GROUND
BLACK PEPPER

Make 10 small incisions over the leg of lamb and stuff each with a piece of garlic and a sprig of rosemary. Drizzle the lamb with a little olive oil, place into a roasting tin and season with a little salt and pepper. Roast for about 30 minutes. Reduce the oven temperature to 180°C/fan 160°C/gas 4. Baste the lamb from time to time and roast for a further 50 minutes or so, depending on how you like your lamb. Remove from the oven, cover with foil and allow the meat to rest for 15 to 20 minutes.

To make the gravy, scoop off most of the fat from the roasting tin. Add the shallots and sauté for about 2 to 3 minutes over a low heat, then add the garlic and cook for 1 minute. Pour in the red wine, tomato purée, honey and stock and simmer for 3 minutes, stirring in the cornflour mix to thicken slightly, and season with salt and freshly ground black pepper.

Serve the lamb on a large platter with roast potatoes, the Moroccan mint jelly and the gravy.

LAMB WELLINGTON WITH WILD GARLIC

Serves 4

Beef Wellington is truly delicious. Being lamb farmers here at Ballyknocken, we adore our family version of Lamb Wellington. It really is a very fine dish, perfect for that 'wow factor' when you really want to impress.

3 TBSP OLIVE OIL

4 X 120G LAMB FILLETS (ASK YOUR BUTCHER TO TRIM THEM FOR YOU)

GOOD PINCH OF PAPRIKA

SALT AND FRESHLY GROUND BLACK PEPPER

3 SHALLOTS, FINELY SLICED

1 GARLIC CLOVE, FINELY SLICED

250G FRESH SEASONAL MIXED MUSHROOMS, SLICED

2 TBSP MADEIRA

50ML WHITE WINE MIXED WITH 1 TSP CORNFLOUR

75G PORK OR DUCK-LIVER PÂTÉ

16 YOUNG WILD GARLIC LEAVES

300G ALL-BUTTER PUFF PASTRY

EGG WASH, TO GLAZE

Heat the oil in a large frying pan over a high heat. Sear 2 pieces of lamb at a time until golden brown all round. Season with paprika, salt and freshly ground black pepper. Leave to cool.

Add the shallots and garlic to the frying pan and sauté for 3 to 4 minutes. Then add the mushrooms and cook for a further 4 to 5 minutes. Deglaze the pan with the Madeira, then add the white wine and cornflour mix and cook until the mixture has thickened. Lastly add the pâté and salt and pepper to taste and allow to cool.

Preheat the oven to 210°C/fan 190°C/gas 7. Line a baking tray with parchment paper.

Wrap 4 wild garlic leaves around each lamb fillet. Roll out the puff pastry to 0.5 cm thick and cut into 4 equal rectangles, each of sufficient size to wrap around a lamb fillet.

Spread a layer of the cold mushroom mix over each rectangle of pastry, leaving a 3cm edge free all the way around. Place a fillet in the middle of each and wrap the puff pastry around it. Brush the edges of the pastry with egg wash and seal well.

Place the wrapped fillets, unsealed side up, on the lined baking tray. Make a small slit in the pastry for the steam to escape during the baking process. Then score the puff pastry on top. Brush with egg wash, making sure that only the tops and sides are coated and that the parchment paper is free of egg wash. Bake for about 17 to 20 minutes until the pastry is golden.

Leave to rest for 4 minutes before cutting so that the juices in the meat can settle. Serve sliced on a platter with Polenta and Parsley Chunky Parsnips (see p. 138).

Wicklow Lamb Steak with Wild Leaves, Mushrooms and a Blackberry Dressing

Serves 4

I made this dish at the lovely Blackstairs Ecotrail Centre, where we foraged for the mushrooms, blackberries, wild mint and leaves. It's amazing the quantity of wild edibles just outside your back door. But, like anything in life, you need to know what you are looking for!

FOR THE LAMB MARINADE

1 LIME, ZEST AND JUICE

60ML RAPESEED OIL, PLUS EXTRA FOR BRUSHING

½ TSP CRUSHED FENNEL SEEDS

1 TSP CHOPPED ROSEMARY

FRESHLY GROUND BLACK PEPPER

4 LAMB STEAKS

FOR THE MUSHROOMS

2 TBSP BUTTER

RAPESEED OIL

200G WILD MUSHROOMS, SLICED

2 SPRIGS OF THYME

2 GARLIC CLOVES, CHOPPED

DASH OF BRANDY (OR BEECH LIQUEUR)

150ML CREAM

SALT AND FRESHLY GROUND BLACK PEPPER

To prepare the marinade, mix the lime, oil, fennel seeds, rosemary and freshly ground black pepper in a large plastic ziplock bag. Place the lamb into the bag, seal and leave to marinate in the fridge for 5 to 6 hours. Remove from the fridge and bring the lamb to room temperature (allow 30 minutes).

For the mushrooms, heat the butter and some oil in large frying pan. Add the mushrooms and thyme. Fry on a high heat, stirring constantly. After a few minutes, add in the garlic. When the mushrooms are cooked, pour in the brandy and cook for a further 1 minute to burn off the alcohol. Then stir in the cream, salt and freshly ground black pepper to taste. Keep warm.

Preheat a chargrill pan over a high heat. Pat the lamb dry, brush with a little oil and season with salt and pepper. Cook first on a high heat on both sides to seal then reduce the heat and continue to cook to your liking – about three minutes each side for medium rare and longer for more well done, depending on the size and thickness of the steaks. Remove from the pan and leave to rest, covered, for about 4 minutes.

Meanwhile, to prepare the dressing, whisk all the ingredients together, except the blackberries. Then add the blackberries and leave to infuse for a few minutes.

To serve, arrange the lamb steaks with the mushrooms and some wild leaves and spoon over the blackberry dressing. Garnish with sprigs of wild mint.

FOR THE DRESSING

50ML OR A LITTLE MORE BALSAMIC VINEGAR

4 TBSP RAPESEED OIL

1 LIME, JUICE ONLY

3 TO 4 TBSP LOCAL HONEY

SALT AND FRESHLY GROUND BLACK PEPPER

200G BLACKBERRIES

120G WILD LEAVES, E.G. DANDELION, BURDOCK, CHICKWEED

4 SMALL SPRIGS OF WILD MINT, TO GARNISH

Chicken Supreme with Spinach and Herb Stuffing and Sorrel Cream Sauce

Serves 4

We serve a version of this country-style dish at our B&B on Friday and Saturday evenings. I often add pancetta or Parmesan to the filling, which gets the Italian part of the family's stamp of approval!

FOR THE FILLING

2 TBSP BUTTER

1 ONION, FINELY CHOPPED

15 BABY SPINACH LEAVES, TRIMMED AND SHREDDED

4 TBSP RICOTTA

$\frac{1}{2}$ LEMON, ZEST ONLY

2 SMALL SPRIGS OF ROSEMARY, FINELY CHOPPED

SALT AND FRESHLY GROUND BLACK PEPPER

4 SUPREMES OF CHICKEN (BREASTS WITH SKIN ON AND WING BONES ATTACHED), TRIMMED

RAPESEED OIL, FOR FRYING AND DRIZZLING

FOR THE DRY RUB

$1\frac{1}{2}$ TSP ONION POWDER

$\frac{1}{2}$ TSP PAPRIKA

1 TSP GARLIC POWDER

$\frac{1}{2}$ TSP CUMIN

2 TSP CHOPPED THYME

$\frac{1}{2}$ TSP SALT

$\frac{1}{4}$ TSP GROUND BLACK PEPPER

To make the filling, melt the butter in a medium saucepan over a medium heat, add the onion and sauté for 5 to 6 minutes until softened but not browned. Take the pan off the heat and add the spinach, ricotta, lemon zest and rosemary and season with salt and freshly ground black pepper. This mix must be cold before you stuff the meat.

Using a sharp knife, make an incision in the side of each chicken supreme, forming a pocket to hold the filling. Using a teaspoon, spread some filling into each pocket.

Preheat the oven to 180°C/fan 160°C/gas 4. Line a roasting tin with parchment paper.

To make the rub, combine all the ingredients in a small bowl and mix well. Rub each chicken supreme with some of the dry rub. Add some oil to a large pan and fry the chicken, skin side only, for a few minutes to colour nicely, then transfer to the roasting tin, drizzle with oil and season with salt and pepper. Sprinkle over the rosemary sprigs.

Roast for about 20 to 25 minutes, depending on the size of the supreme of chicken. Check that the chicken is cooked – when the meat is pierced, the juices should run clear.

Meanwhile, to make the sauce, heat the oil in the frying pan that was used to brown the chicken, thereby gathering all the lovely caramelised juices for the sauce. Add the onion and sauté until softened but not browned. This will take about 5 to 6 minutes. Add the garlic and cook for about 1 minute. Pour in the white wine and simmer for a few minutes, then stir in the sorrel, vegetable stock and cream and simmer for another 2 to 3 minutes.

Pour the sauce into a blender (or use a handheld one) and purée until smooth. Return to the saucepan and heat through. Check the seasoning, adding salt and freshly ground black pepper as needed. If the sauce is too thick, add a little vegetable stock.

To serve at a dinner party, place all the supremes of chicken on a long platter and spoon the sauce over the top. Garnish with sprigs of rosemary.

To serve on single plates, cut a few slices from each supreme and then place the slices with the rest of the supreme on a plate. Serve with mashed potato with some sautéed leeks folded through and the sorrel sauce spooned over the chicken. Garnish with sprigs of rosemary and serve immediately.

FOR THE SAUCE

1 TBSP RAPESEED OIL

1 ONION, FINELY SLICED

1 GARLIC CLOVE, FINELY CHOPPED

75ML WHITE WINE

8 LARGE FRENCH SORREL LEAVES, SHREDDED

75ML VEGETABLE STOCK

150ML CREAM

SALT AND FRESHLY GROUND BLACK PEPPER

SMALL SPRIGS OF ROSEMARY, TO GARNISH

Italian-Style Tomato, Shallot and Rosemary Chicken Hotpot

Serves 4

One-pot wonders are the solution to healthy, nutritious meals in our busy lives. This one is packed with vegetables and, because I'm using chicken thighs, it freezes very well also.

FOR THE HOTPOT

OLIVE OIL, FOR FRYING

8 DEBONED, SKINLESS CHICKEN THIGHS

SALT AND FRESHLY GROUND BLACK PEPPER

8 SHALLOTS, PEELED AND HALVED

2 GARLIC CLOVES, FINELY CHOPPED

1 MEDIUM CARROT, FINELY DICED

1 TSP CHOPPED ROSEMARY

2 TSP CHOPPED OREGANO

400G TINNED DICED TOMATOES

1 TSP HONEY

500ML CHICKEN STOCK

12 BLACK OLIVES, PITTED

FOR THE POTATO AND PARMESAN TOPPING

4 POTATOES, PEELED AND THINLY SLICED

1 TBSP MELTED BUTTER MIXED WITH 1 TBSP OLIVE OIL

3 TBSP GRATED PARMESAN

2 TSP CHOPPED MIXED ROSEMARY AND OREGANO

Heat a little oil in a casserole dish over a medium heat. Season the chicken thighs with salt and freshly ground black pepper and sear until golden brown. Place on a clean plate and set aside.

Add the shallots and sauté for about 4 minutes, until golden, before adding the garlic and cooking for 1 minute. Then add the carrot, rosemary and oregano as well as the tomatoes, honey and chicken stock. Bring to the boil and check for seasoning, adding salt and pepper as required.

Preheat the oven to 180°C/fan 160°C/gas 4.

Return the chicken thighs to the casserole dish, stir well and add the olives.

For the topping, arrange the potato slices neatly over the top of the hotpot, starting from the outer edge and leaving a small space in the centre. Brush the potato slices with the melted butter and oil mix and sprinkle the Parmesan and chopped herbs on top.

Bake in the oven for about 30 to 35 minutes until the potatoes are cooked and golden. Leave to settle for 5 minutes, then sprinkle a little salt over the top before serving.

Sicilian Lemony Roast Chicken and Potatoes

Serves 4

This is one of my favourites from a little 'takeaway' that we love to visit in the seaside town of Ballestrate in Sicily. It's such a great family-style recipe and you can add to it to suit your tastes – I sometimes add pancetta or chorizo; other times I add olives and sun-dried tomatoes.

6 LARGE POTATOES, PEELED AND ROUGHLY QUARTERED

EXTRA VIRGIN OLIVE OIL, FOR ROASTING

4 GARLIC CLOVES, SLICED

2 LEMONS: 1 JUICED AND ZESTED; THE OTHER SLICED INTO 6 WEDGES

7 SPRIGS OF ROSEMARY

6 SMALL SPRIGS OF OREGANO

SALT AND FRESHLY GROUND BLACK PEPPER

1 LARGE CORN-FED CHICKEN, PORTIONED (ASK YOUR BUTCHER TO DO THIS FOR YOU)

3 TBSP PLAIN FLOUR, SEASONED WITH 1 TSP LEMON ZEST, $\frac{1}{2}$ TSP PAPRIKA AND $\frac{1}{4}$ TSP SALT

Preheat the oven to 190°C/fan 170°C/gas 5.

To a shallow medium-sized roasting tin, add the potatoes, a generous amount of olive oil, the garlic, lemon juice, zest and wedges and sprigs of rosemary and oregano. Season with salt and freshly ground black pepper. Toss the potatoes well in the mix then roast for about 20 minutes.

Dust the chicken portions in the seasoned flour. Heat a large frying pan with some oil. Add the chicken portions and brown on all sides.

Arrange the chicken on top of the potatoes. Season with salt and freshly ground black pepper and baste with the lemon oil from the roasting tray. Return to the oven and roast for a further 25 minutes or so until the chicken is fully cooked. The juices must run clear from the chicken.

Serve with a garden salad of baby spinach leaves, orange segments and a light dressing of orange juice and extra virgin olive oil.

WICKLOW WOLF BRAISED BEEF

Serves 6

We have such a wealth of choice in Ireland when it comes to artisan beers. Here I'm using our local Wicklow Wolf Black Perle Porter. I'm sure there are many who would say it's best chilled in a glass but it works really well in this recipe too!

RAPESEED OIL

1.5KG ROUND-STEAK ROASTING JOINT

SALT AND FRESHLY GROUND BLACK PEPPER

2 ONIONS, SLICED

3 CARROTS, PEELED AND SLICED

BOUQUET GARNI (SPRIGS OF BAY TREE, SAGE, ROSEMARY, OREGANO AND THYME, TIED WITH STRING)

5 GARLIC CLOVES, HALVED

¼ TSP DRIED CHILLI FLAKES

1 TBSP WHOLEGRAIN MUSTARD

1 TSP HONEY

2 TSP WORCESTERSHIRE SAUCE

1 PINT WICKLOW WOLF BLACK PERLE PORTER

100ML BEEF STOCK

FOR THE GRAVY

1 TBSP CORNFLOUR

250ML BEEF STOCK (YOU MAY NEED A LITTLE MORE)

Preheat the oven to 180°C/fan 160°C/gas 4.

Heat a little oil in a large casserole dish over a medium heat. Season the beef with salt and freshly ground black pepper and then sear on all sides. Lift out and place on a clean plate.

Add the onions and carrots to the casserole dish, together with the bouquet garni and garlic, and fry until the onions have softened. Add the chilli flakes, mustard, honey, Worcestershire sauce, porter and beef stock and stir well.

Return the beef to the casserole dish. Cover with a lid or a piece of foil and transfer to the preheated oven.

Once the beef is done as much as you want (the general rule is 15 minutes per 450g for medium), lift it out of the casserole dish, place in a clean dish, cover and leave to rest for about 20 minutes.

To make the gravy, remove the bouquet garni, skim the excess fat from the braising juices and mash in the vegetables. Mix the cornflour with 3 tbsp of the beef stock then add it, along with the remaining beef stock, to the dish and heat. Whisk until the gravy thickens then pour into a jug.

Place the beef on a board and slice thinly. Serve with Garlic and Rosemary Roast Potatoes (see p. 136) and some gravy poured over.

Beef and Stout Pies with Potato Pastry Topping

Makes about 6, depending on the size

I'm bragging now, but this recipe was the winner in a live TV cook-off on the NBC *Today Show*. The potato pastry was what helped clinch the prize! It's a wonderful Irish-heritage recipe that was passed on to me.

FOR THE FILLING

RAPESEED OIL, FOR SAUTÉING

100G SMOKED BACON, SLICED INTO LARDONS

1KG ROUND STEAK STEWING BEEF, DICED

PLAIN FLOUR, SEASONED WITH SALT AND PEPPER

1 LARGE ONION, THINLY SLICED

500ML STOUT

1 RED PEPPER, DICED

400G TINNED DICED TOMATOES

1½ TBSP TOMATO PURÉE

2 TSP SUGAR

¾ TSP ENGLISH MUSTARD POWDER

BOUQUET GARNI (4 TO 5 PARSLEY SPRIGS, 1 FRESH THYME SPRIG AND 1 BAY LEAF, TIED TOGETHER)

SALT AND FRESHLY GROUND BLACK PEPPER

Heat some oil in a casserole dish over a medium heat. Add the bacon and sauté until crispy. Transfer to a clean plate and set aside.

Toss the diced beef in the seasoned flour and dust off the excess. Add a little more oil to the casserole dish and fry the beef in batches until browned on all sides. Place the seared beef pieces on the clean plate with the bacon and set aside.

Add a little more oil to the casserole dish and gently sauté the onion until just softened but not browned. Deglaze the pan with some stout.

Return the beef, bacon and their juices to the casserole dish and stir in the red pepper, tomatoes, tomato purée, sugar, mustard and bouquet garni and season with salt and freshly ground black pepper.

Add the rest of the stout. Bring to the boil, cover, reduce the heat and then simmer over a low heat for about 1½ hours or until the meat is tender and the sauce thick, stirring from time to time.

Meanwhile, prepare the pastry. Sift the flour and salt into a large bowl. Add the diced butter and rub with your fingertips until the mixture resembles fine breadcrumbs. Add the baking powder and mix well. Stir in the potatoes and pour in just enough cold water to form a soft dough. Turn it out on a floured surface and knead very lightly. Wrap in clingfilm and leave to rest for 30 minutes in the fridge. (The pastry can also be made several hours in advance and stored in the fridge until you're ready to use it.)

FOR THE PASTRY

170G PLAIN FLOUR, PLUS
EXTRA FOR DUSTING

½ TSP SALT

115G CHILLED BUTTER,
DICED

¾ TSP BAKING
POWDER

150G STEAMED POTATOES,
PRESSED THROUGH A
RICER

COLD WATER (ABOUT 3
TBSP), TO BIND

EGG WASH

200G CHESTNUT (OR
ANY OF YOUR FAVOURITE)
MUSHROOMS, CLEANED
AND SLICED

1 TBSP BUTTER

During the last 10 minutes of the filling's cooking time, heat a medium frying pan with a little butter, add the mushrooms with some salt and freshly ground black pepper and sauté for about 4 to 5 minutes. Then add to the casserole and simmer for 3 to 4 minutes. Check the seasoning, adding more salt and pepper if required.

When you are ready to make the pies, remove the bouquet garni from the beef.

Choose 6 ramekins (or more, depending on their size). Preheat the oven to 210°C/fan 190°C/gas 7.

Carefully roll out the pastry on a floured surface – it shouldn't be too thin. Using a large cutter, cut out 6 or more discs 2cm larger than the ramekins. Spoon the beef into the bowls, brush the edges with egg wash and place the pastry discs on top. Crimp the edges. Re-roll the pastry trimmings and use to cut out leaves. Attach these to the top of the pies with egg wash. Make a small hole in the top of each disc for the steam to escape.

Leave in the fridge to rest for about 20 minutes. Then brush the pastry with egg wash and transfer the ramekins to the oven for about 18 to 20 minutes or until the pastry is golden and baked.

Rest for about 5 minutes before serving with a fresh garden salad.

PEPPERED SIRLOIN STEAK WITH WHISKEY CREAM SAUCE

Serves 2

The most important factor, I feel, when cooking steak (and it doesn't matter what you use – a frying pan, chargrill pan or barbecue) is that it's rested after cooking. I often get asked if the meat will go cold and, honestly, the answer is that, as long as you wrap it loosely in foil, it doesn't. And don't forget to pour any juices that run during resting time back into your sauces for maximum flavour.

1 GARLIC CLOVE, SLICED IN HALF

2 X 170G SIRLOIN STEAKS

RAPESEED OIL, FOR BRUSHING

SALT AND FRESHLY GROUND BLACK PEPPER

1 TBSP BUTTER

FOR THE SAUCE

4 TBSP WHISKEY

2 TSP CRUSHED PEPPERCORNS

100ML CHICKEN OR BEEF STOCK

150ML DOUBLE CREAM

1/2 TSP FINELY CHOPPED THYME

Rub one half of the garlic clove over the steaks and thinly slice the other half. Brush the steaks with a little oil and sprinkle over salt and freshly ground black pepper.

Heat a large frying pan over a medium to high heat. Place the steaks in the pan and cook for 1½ to 2½ minutes on each side, sealing them well. The guidelines are: for rare 1½ minutes on each side; for medium rare 2 minutes on each side; for medium 2½ minutes on each side; and for well-done 3 minutes on each side. There will be variables, though, such as the temperature of the hob, the thickness of the steak etc. When the meat is just cooked to your liking, add the butter and allow to foam, basting the steak with it. Remove the steaks and allow to rest for 5 minutes, covered with foil.

To make the sauce, deglaze the pan with whiskey, then flambé to burn off the alcohol, thereby removing the sharp flavour. To do this, remove the pan from the heat and add the whiskey. If using a gas hob, slightly tip the pan to let the flame catch the whiskey and ignite. Immediately lay the pan flat on the gas, reduce the heat and wait for the flames to burn down. Do stand back during this process! If using an electric hob, you will need a long-handled lighter to ignite the alcohol. Flambéing is quite dramatic, but do be careful of the high flames. Never pour alcohol directly from a bottle when using a gas flame and always measure correctly. Too much alcohol will result in very high flames.

Alternatively, you can let the alcohol boil off. The flavour will be slightly different but equally tasty.

Once you've done this, add the crushed peppercorns, sliced garlic, stock, cream and thyme. Stir well and check the seasoning. Simmer the sauce for a few minutes until it coats the back of a spoon.

Transfer the steaks to warm serving plates, spoon over the sauce and serve immediately with steamed potatoes and wilted kale.

Rosemary, Apple and Celery-Stuffed Pork Chops
with Apple Cider Sauce

Serves 4

Here's a lovely little recipe from our 30-Minute Mains cookery class. These pork chops are a great midweek dinner: the stuffing and sauce are simple to put together and if you ask your butcher to make the pockets in the chops, then it couldn't be easier.

FOR THE STUFFING

OLIVE OIL, FOR FRYING

1 CELERY STICK, FINELY DICED

3 SHALLOTS, FINELY SLICED

1 MEDIUM APPLE, PEELED AND DICED INTO SMALL PIECES

1 TSP CHOPPED ROSEMARY

1 TBSP PARSLEY, CHOPPED

SALT AND FRESHLY GROUND BLACK PEPPER, TO TASTE

4 PORK CHOPS (ASK YOUR BUTCHER TO TRIM THEM)

2 TBSP RAPESEED OIL

FOR THE SAUCE

3 TSP WHOLEGRAIN MUSTARD

150ML APPLE CIDER

100ML VEGETABLE STOCK

3 TBSP CRÈME FRAÎCHE

2 TSP CHOPPED ROSEMARY

SALT AND FRESHLY GROUND BLACK PEPPER

4 ROSEMARY SPRIGS, TO GARNISH

To prepare the stuffing, first heat some olive oil in a large frying pan. Sauté the celery and shallots until softened but not browned, then add the apple and rosemary and sauté for a further 2 minutes. Add the parsley and check the seasoning, adding salt and freshly ground black pepper to taste. Leave to cool.

Make an incision, or pocket, in the side of each chop and season with salt and freshly ground black pepper. Spread some cold stuffing into each pocket and pin with a cocktail stick or a large, strong rosemary sprig if you feel that you need to secure it.

Heat the rapeseed oil in a large frying pan over a medium heat. Place the chops into the pan and fry for about 4 minutes on each side – check that they are cooked through. Remove the chops to a warm plate and keep warm, allowing them to rest for about 5 minutes.

In the meantime, make the sauce. Pour off the excess oil from the frying pan, stir in the mustard and add the cider, stock, crème fraîche and rosemary. Simmer gently for about 3 minutes until the sauce thickens. Season with salt and freshly ground pepper to taste.

To serve, spoon some mash with finely shredded Swiss chard folded through onto each plate. Arrange a pork chop on top and spoon over some sauce. Drizzle a little extra sauce around the plate and garnish with a few rosemary sprigs.

STUFFED DATE AND HAZELNUT PORK FILLET
WITH CREAMY MUSHROOM AND PINK PEPPERCORN SAUCE

Serves 4

We had this on a family trip to Wexford. Claudio liked it so much, he ordered the same again on the second night of our stay! When he got home, he tried to recreate it, so this is now also known as 'Dad's Pork' in our house. We've also made it with diced dried apricots and even fresh pears when in season, and it's still much loved.

600G PORK FILLET, TRIMMED

10 STRIPS OF PANCETTA

SALT AND FRESHLY GROUND BLACK PEPPER

FOR THE STUFFING

8 MEDJOOL OR READY-TO-EAT DATES, PITTED AND ROUGHLY CHOPPED

2 TSP CHOPPED THYME

75G BREADCRUMBS

½ LEMON, ZEST ONLY

4 TBSP TOASTED HAZELNUTS, CHOPPED

SPRIGS OF THYME AND 4 BAY LEAVES

RAPESEED OIL

FOR THE SAUCE

150G YOUR FAVOURITE MUSHROOM SELECTION, SLICED

2 TBSP BRANDY

6 SMALL SPRIGS OF THYME

1 TSP PINK PEPPERCORNS, CRUSHED

220ML DOUBLE CREAM

SALT AND FRESHLY GROUND BLACK PEPPER

SPRIGS OF THYME, TO GARNISH

Preheat the oven to 180°C/fan 160°C/gas 4.

To prepare the pork fillet, make an incision along the top but not cutting all the way through the meat. Lay the pancetta in strips underneath the pork. Season the meat with salt and freshly ground black pepper.

To make the stuffing, place the dates, thyme, breadcrumbs, lemon zest and hazelnuts into a small bowl and mix well.

Spoon the mix into the incision in the fillet. Then lift and cross the pancetta strips over the meat.

Place the sprigs of thyme and the bay leaves on top and tie 3 pieces of string around the fillet – one near each end and one in the middle – to secure the filling.

To cook, heat some rapeseed oil in a casserole dish over a high heat and brown the pork on all sides. Transfer to the oven and roast for about 35 to 40 minutes or until the fillet is cooked through. Remove, cover loosely with foil and leave to rest.

To make the sauce, place the casserole dish back on the hob, then add the mushrooms, brandy and thyme sprigs and sauté until the mushrooms are just cooked. Add the peppercorns and sauté for 1 minute before pouring in the cream. Leave to simmer for about 2 minutes. Check the seasoning, adding salt and freshly ground black pepper as needed.

To serve, slice the pork fillet and place a few slices on each serving plate. Spoon over some mushroom sauce and serve with potatoes roasted with a little thyme and baked sweet potato wedges.

Ham Croquettes with Leek and Paprika Sauce

Makes 12

A firm favourite with my children, these have meat and veg in them so all boxes are ticked! It's also quite a useful recipe for using up leftovers. The beauty of croquettes is that the filling can be changed to suit what's in the fridge – I often add diced, sautéed chorizo or smoked salmon. Sometimes I even make smaller ones to serve as canapés with drinks in summer in the herb garden.

FOR THE CROQUETTES

100G GOOD QUALITY HAM, DICED INTO SMALL PIECES

350G WARM MASHED POTATO

GOOD HANDFUL YOUNG SPINACH, SHREDDED

1/2 LEMON, ZEST ONLY

1 TBSP CHOPPED CHIVES

2 TSP CHOPPED OREGANO

3 TBSP PLAIN FLOUR, SEASONED WITH SALT AND FRESHLY GROUND BLACK PEPPER

1 EGG, BEATEN

4 TBSP FRESH BREADCRUMBS

3 TBSP SESAME SEEDS

RAPESEED OIL, FOR FRYING

FOR THE SAUCE

RAPESEED OIL, FOR FRYING

1/2 MEDIUM LEEK, FINELY SLICED

2 TSP WHOLEGRAIN MUSTARD

1/2 TSP SWEET PAPRIKA

4 TBSP CRÈME FRAÎCHE

1 TSP CHOPPED OREGANO

1 TBSP CHOPPED PARSLEY

100ML VEGETABLE STOCK

SALT AND FRESHLY GROUND BLACK PEPPER

To make the croquettes, place the ham, potato, spinach, lemon zest, chives and oregano in a medium-sized bowl and mix together. Divide into 12 portions to shape.

Spoon the seasoned flour out onto a clean plate. Pour the beaten egg into a shallow, wide bowl, and spread the breadcrumbs and sesame seeds out on a clean plate.

Dampen your hands with cold water and shape the ham-and-potato mixture into croquettes. Dip each one into the egg, roll in the flour, then the breadcrumbs and place on a plate lined with parchment paper. Leave in the fridge for half an hour to set.

To make the sauce, heat some oil in a saucepan over a medium heat, add the leek and sauté for 5 to 6 minutes until softened but not browned. Stir in the mustard, paprika, crème fraîche, oregano and parsley. Pour in the stock and simmer to thicken slightly, then season with salt and freshly ground black pepper to taste.

To cook the croquettes, heat some oil in a large frying pan over a medium heat. Carefully place the croquettes in the frying pan in batches and fry until golden and crispy and heated through.

To serve, place some wilted chard on a platter, arrange the croquettes on top and spoon over some of the sauce – serve the rest in a small ramekin on the side.

ROSEMARY VENISON WITH SHALLOT AND RED WINE SAUCE

Serves 6

Wrapping a joint of meat is such an impressive way to roast it yet keep all the flavours in. In fact, using buttered paper and a paste of flour and water is a very old way of roasting. I have seen recipes dating back to the early 1800s recommending this method of cooking for wild fowl and venison. It doesn't take too much time and it's a bit like making a papier mâché parcel. This is by far my favourite venison recipe!

FOR THE STUFFING

200G RAW CHORIZO

2 SAGE LEAVES, FINELY CHOPPED

10 DRIED APRICOT HALVES, FINELY CHOPPED

1 LARGE ONION, FINELY CHOPPED

BUTTER FOR GREASING

LEG OF VENISON, DEBONED AND BUTTERFLIED (ASK YOUR BUTCHER TO DO THIS FOR YOU)

RAPESEED OIL, FOR BRUSHING

FOR THE RUB

1 TBSP JUNIPER BERRIES

5 SPRIGS OF ROSEMARY

2 GARLIC CLOVES

2 TSP SEA SALT

2 SAGE LEAVES, CHOPPED

2 TSP BLACK PEPPERCORNS

FOR THE PASTE

1KG PLAIN FLOUR

1.2L COLD WATER

FOR THE SAUCE

2 TBSP BUTTER

5 SHALLOTS, SLICED

½ TSP GROUND JUNIPER BERRIES

1 TSP DIJON-STYLE MUSTARD

1 TSP CHOPPED ROSEMARY

1 TBSP CORNFLOUR

400ML RED WINE

SALT AND FRESHLY GROUND BLACK PEPPER

Preheat the oven to 170°C/fan 150°C/gas 3. Generously butter two large pieces of parchment paper on one side. Combine all the ingredients for the stuffing and season with salt and freshly ground black pepper. Then stuff the butterflied venison and tie with string. Brush with oil.

Place all the ingredients for the rub into a mortar and grind with a pestle. Rub the spices over the meat. Wrap one piece of the parchment paper, butter-side facing the meat, around the venison.

To make the paste, place the flour in a large bowl and add enough water to form a thick paste when mixed.

Coat the parchment-wrapped venison in the paste. Wrap the other piece of buttered parchment paper over and secure with string. Place in a large roasting tin to bake/roast for about 3½ hours. Remove from the oven and allow to rest for 30 minutes.

To make the sauce, heat the butter in a saucepan over a medium heat, then add the shallots and sauté until softened but not browned. Add the juniper berries, mustard, rosemary and cornflour and sauté for 2 minutes. Pour in the wine and simmer for a further 5 minutes until the sauce thickens. Season with salt and freshly ground black pepper to taste.

To serve, unwrap the venison and carve into slices. Spoon the red wine sauce over and serve with a generous portion of roast potatoes.

FIVE-SPICE SEARED DUCK BREASTS
WITH HONEY AND RASPBERRY SAUCE AND WILTED PAK CHOI AND SPRING ONIONS

Serves 4

For a good few years now, I've been able to grow pak choi in our vegetable garden. Having grown up with a vegetable patch full of the old reliables – turnips, carrots, potatoes and the like – pak choi seems delightfully exotic. It's amazing what the climate in Ireland can produce!

4 X 200G DUCK BREASTS, SKIN ON

1 TSP FIVE-SPICE POWDER

SALT AND FRESHLY GROUND BLACK PEPPER

FOR THE SAUCE

1 TBSP BUTTER

1 ORANGE, ZEST AND JUICE

2CM FRESH ROOT GINGER, GRATED

3 TBSP HONEY

200G RASPBERRIES

FOR THE VEGETABLES

RAPESEED OIL, FOR SAUTÉING

1 RED CHILLI, FINELY SLICED

1/2 TSP GROUND CUMIN

6 SPRING ONIONS, TRIMMED AND SLICED LENGTHWAYS INTO 3

2 PAK CHOI, TRIMMED AND SLICED LENGTHWAYS

BUNCH OF CORIANDER, CHOPPED

To prepare the duck, score the duck breasts diagonally each way with a sharp knife and rub with the five-spice powder, salt and freshly ground black pepper.

Place the duck, skin side down, into a large cold frying pan and leave to cook slowly on a low heat until the skin is golden and the duck fat has melted into the pan. Turn the duck breasts over, increase the heat to medium and cook for a further 5 minutes approximately, until tender but still pink in the middle. Remove from the pan, cover and keep warm.

To make the sauce, heat the butter in a saucepan over a medium heat. Add the orange juice and zest and simmer for 2 minutes before adding the ginger, honey and raspberries. Simmer for 2 minutes and set aside.

To prepare the vegetables, heat some oil in a large frying pan over a high heat. Add the red chilli, cumin and spring onions and sauté for 1 minute before adding the pak choi and sautéing for a further 2 to 3 minutes. Stir in the chopped coriander.

To serve, place the wilted spring onions and pak choi on a large platter, then slice the duck and arrange the slices on top. Spoon over the raspberry sauce and serve immediately.

Winter Rabbit Casserole

Serves 4 to 6

Rabbit is very popular in Sicily, where my husband is from, and my dad often tells of how he enjoyed my grandmother's rabbit stew. It's something that has lost popularity in Ireland but seems to be making a comeback. Many butchers stock rabbit nowadays. If rabbit isn't to your liking, try this recipe with chicken or pork.

2 RABBITS, PORTIONED (ASK YOUR BUTCHER TO DO THIS)

2 TBSP FLOUR, SEASONED WITH SALT, FRESHLY GROUND BLACK PEPPER AND 1/4 TSP OF CUMIN

RAPESEED OIL, FOR FRYING

100G SMOKED BACON, DICED

1 ONION, DICED

2 GARLIC CLOVES, CHOPPED

3 MEDIUM SPRIGS OF ROSEMARY

1 CELERY STICK, SLICED

1 YELLOW PEPPER, DESEEDED AND SLICED

2 BAY LEAVES

250ML PEAR CIDER

300ML VEGETABLE STOCK

SALT AND FRESHLY GROUND BLACK PEPPER

1 PEAR, SLICED INTO THIN WEDGES AND SAUTÉED IN A LITTLE BUTTER, TO GARNISH

BAY LEAVES, TO GARNISH

Dust the rabbit portions in the seasoned flour. Heat some oil in a casserole dish over a medium heat and add the rabbit portions. Sear on all sides and set aside on a clean plate.

Add the bacon to the casserole dish and cook until crispy. Transfer to a clean plate.

Heat a little more oil and add the onion, garlic, rosemary and celery and sauté for about 3 minutes.

Stir the yellow pepper slices and bay leaves into the casserole and cook for 5 minutes before adding the pear cider and cooking for a further 5 minutes. Return the rabbit to the casserole and pour over the vegetable stock. Season with salt and freshly ground black pepper and simmer slowly for about 1 hour, stirring from time to time.

Serve with Mustard and Spinach Mash (see p. 135) and some pear wedges on top, garnished with bay leaves.

THE GREAT VEG PLOT

Sides and Salads

When I first established our raised beds, I didn't realise or even dream that we would have a garden that would produce so much – and it is so satisfying. We've an abundance of easy-to-grow vegetables and then fields beyond to forage in. There's something very special about home-grown produce – apart from doing the picking yourself, there's the achievement of growing them, the fresh flavours and, of course, the health benefits. One thing I know is that almost every vegetable is even more delicious with added flavour, and that's important to me when planning dinners for guests in our B&B. We always try to offer interesting and tasty vegetables. During autumn, we enjoy rainbow chard, celeriac, beetroot, savoy and red cabbages, cauliflower, broccoli, kale, celery (which seems to grow forever), the reliable leeks, parsnips, purple sprouting broccoli, potatoes, those knobbly ones – the Jerusalem artichokes! – and chard. The spring brings sorrel. The kale is still around and the new spinach leaves are popping through. Lettuce leaves (like frilly red sail, blushed butter oak, speckled butterhead and textured cos), leeks, beetroot, wild garlic and dandelions all start to appear. In the summer, we'll have pak choi, chop suey, our endless supply of courgettes (including the treat of a courgette flower dusted with flour and fried), all the 'cut and come again' salad leaves, like rocket and mizuna, artichokes, broad beans, wigwams of French beans, a few rows of radishes, mangetout (sugar snap peas), spring onions and watercress. I'm sure I'm forgetting lots, but it really is a joy to see the garden produce. And we can pick as we need, so there is no wastage.

How to ...
Make the Most of Vegetables

Apparently, as consumers, we waste quite a lot of vegetables every year. I have a theory about that. I believe that we undertake our 'big shop' once a week, during which we purchase sufficient to last us seven days. And with our virtuous and healthy ambitions for the week ahead, we buy more vegetables, as they are so good for our health, than we will realistically ever eat. And so, by the end of the week, these lovely vegetables are wilting and unappetising. I'm always on a mission, in our cookery school and for my family, to make the most of these delicious vegetables, so here are some of my tips to preserve them for longer.

Freezing

I tend to freeze a lot – my freezers are always jammers – and I'm asked regularly how best to freeze vegetables. I do this when they're at their peak or I have a glut. For vegetables like carrots, brussels sprouts, cabbages, asparagus, peas and courgettes, first wash and slice them. Then blanch by adding them to rapidly boiling water to cook for 3 minutes. Refresh by putting them straight into cold water – this keeps the colour vibrant and stops the cooking process – and then drain. Portion them out into ziplock bags, and, of course, label and date them. They are now ready to be frozen. Peppers and chillies can be washed, chopped and frozen without being blanched first.

Pickling

Pickling is another helpful method. It's important to maintain a balance between sweet and sour, smoothness and texture, so I taste regularly towards the end of the cooking process, as some vegetables can be a bit bland, even watery, and others can be sharper, depending on the season. To pickle, you will need equal parts cider vinegar and water and some salt. I also add in some extra spices such as peppercorns or caraway, mustard or coriander seeds. Place the vegetables you want to pickle – onions, beetroot or cucumbers work well – in sterilised jars (see p.133). Add the spices. Bring the water, cider and salt to the boil and pour over the vegetables. Tap to ensure there are no air bubbles and seal with a lid. Keep refrigerated. Enjoy with barbecued foods, homemade burgers, spicy foods and in sandwiches or salads.

STERILISING

When pickling or making preserves, it's essential that your jars are thoroughly sterilised. There are two ways to do this. One, just place them on the top shelf of your dishwasher and run through on your hottest cycle. Or, two, wash them in hot, soapy water, rinse and then place in a preheated oven (130°C/fan 110°C/gas 1) for 10 minutes. Remember to use tongs to lift them out – otherwise: ouch!

CARAMELISED ONIONS

Caramelised onions are such a useful item to have in the fridge. To make them, all you do is slice 4 onions, then heat 3 tbsp of extra virgin olive oil in a saucepan over a low heat, add the onions with about 3 tsp caster sugar and sauté slowly for 10 to 12 minutes, stirring from time to time. Serve with a cheeseboard, add to gravy or enjoy on toast with poached eggs or in sandwiches and salads.

TOMATO PASSATA

Towards the end of summer when there is an oversupply of lovely ripe tomatoes, I make passata and freeze it. You'll need 12 large, ripe tomatoes, 1 tbsp chopped basil, 1 tbsp tomato purée and 3 sun-dried tomato halves. Put all those into a blender and purée until smooth. Heat a little oil in a medium saucepan over a medium heat, add 3 finely chopped cloves of garlic and sauté for 1 to 2 minutes. Pour the puréed tomatoes into the saucepan and simmer slowly for about 12 minutes. Ladle the passata back into the blender and blend until smooth. Season with salt and freshly ground black pepper and then use the back of a spoon to push it through a sieve.

ACCOMPANIMENTS

A good herb oil spooned over hot vegetables is a wonderful addition. To make a herb-infused oil, use the best quality extra virgin olive oil you can get and the freshest of herbs. Wash the herbs and leave to dry fully – at least overnight – then bruise them. Fill a sterilised jar or bottle with the oil and the herbs, seal and leave for about a week for the flavours to infuse. Keep refrigerated or in a cool, dark place to protect against spoilage. The oil should last for a few weeks. If you would like the oil to stay fresher for longer, it's possible to bring the herbs and the oil to the boil to sterilise, but it does affect the flavours somewhat. Flavoured butters also add a new dimension to vegetables (see p. 224).

THE PERFECT SALAD
AND THE PERFECT CROUTONS

I have a formula that I stick to when creating a salad. First I use as many different salad leaves as I can get hold of for colour and texture. Then I'll add a protein, such as chargrilled chicken, prawns or flaked salmon, and some crunch – for that I use flavoured rustic croutons. Sometimes I also add a little sweetness, which could be strawberries, pear wedges or slices of mango – and all this is in addition to things like cucumber ribbons, slices of avocado, thinly sliced fennel and herbs such as dill, mint and chives. For my rustic croutons, I use 1 medium sourdough loaf, roughly torn (these are rustic!), 1½ tsp cumin seeds, 2 tbsp finely chopped parsley, 2 tbsp melted butter and 1 tbsp rapeseed oil. Preheat the oven to 190°C/fan 170°C/gas 5. Place the bread pieces into a large bowl, add the cumin seeds and parsley and pour over the melted butter and oil. Mix well and spoon onto a parchment-lined baking tray. Bake for about 7 minutes, turning once, until golden brown. Keep an eye on them – they tend to burn very quickly! Cooled leftover croutons can be frozen or will keep in an airtight container at room temperature for 2 days.

BALLYKNOCKEN DAUPHINOISE

Serves 6 to 8

I sometimes take a shortcut with this recipe by gently simmering the sliced potatoes in a saucepan with the hot cream and stock for about 15 minutes, until they're just about cooked. Then I arrange them in the gratin dish with the garlic and pancetta or other flavours of choice layered between. I pour over the hot cream and stock and transfer to the oven for about 20 to 25 minutes. It isn't quite the same as the more traditional recipe below, as it's the long, slow cooking time which allows the garlic to infuse into all the layers, but it's handy when the oven is needed for other dishes!

EXTRA VIRGIN OLIVE OIL, FOR SAUTÉING

4 PANCETTA STRIPS, CUT INTO LARDONS

MELTED BUTTER, FOR BRUSHING

50ML VEGETABLE STOCK

500ML CREAM

PINCH OF NUTMEG

SALT AND FRESHLY GROUND BLACK PEPPER

1.5KG POTATOES, PEELED AND SLICED THINLY (A MANDOLINE WOULD BE GOOD FOR THIS)

3 GARLIC CLOVES, THINLY SLICED

50G BUTTER

3 TBSP GRATED PARMESAN

Heat a medium frying pan with a little olive oil, add the pancetta and sauté until crispy. Remove from the pan and place on kitchen paper to drain. Set aside.

Preheat the oven to 180°C /fan 160°C/gas 4. Brush a medium-sized gratin dish with melted butter.

Cover a baking tray with foil and place under the gratin dish (this saves a mess in your oven if the filling bubbles over).

In a saucepan on the hob, warm the stock, cream and nutmeg and add salt and freshly ground black pepper to taste.

Arrange some potato slices in a layer in the gratin dish with some of the pancetta and slices of garlic on top. Layer more potato slices over this, with the pancetta and garlic, and continue to the top of the gratin dish. Pour over the warm cream – it should come to about 1cm below the top layer of potatoes (so add more if necessary). Dot with butter and sprinkle over the Parmesan.

Transfer to the preheated oven. Check every 15 minutes or so and, using the back of a spatula, press the potatoes down slightly so they submerge under the hot cream. Leave to bake until golden brown and cooked through. This will take about 1 hour.

Leave to settle for 5 minutes before serving.

MUSTARD AND SPINACH MASH

Serves 4

The nation's staple is mash so it has to be done right – no lumps! – and that means getting yourself a potato ricer: it's the best gadget that I have in my kitchen.

7 MEDIUM POTATOES, PEELED AND ROUGHLY DICED

100ML MILK

3 TBSP BUTTER

1 TSP WHOLEGRAIN MUSTARD

SALT AND FRESHLY GROUND BLACK PEPPER

GENEROUS HANDFUL YOUNG SPINACH LEAVES, ROUGHLY SHREDDED

Place the diced potatoes into a steamer and cook until softened: this will take about 15 to 18 minutes. While still hot, press the potatoes through a potato ricer.

Heat the milk, butter, mustard, salt and freshly ground black pepper together. (If you do this in a microwave, it will save time.)

Pour the hot milk and butter over the potatoes and fold in gently. The mix should be soft, so add more milk if necessary. Check the seasoning, adding salt and freshly ground black pepper as required. Fold in the roughly chopped spinach.

Ideally it should be served immediately, but you can keep it warm for about 30 minutes over a bain marie. To do this, spoon the mash into a bowl, cover and place over a saucepan of barely simmering water.

GARLIC AND ROSEMARY ROAST POTATOES

Serves a very generous 4 – we love spuds!

In my opinion, Golden Wonders and Roosters make the best roasties. The perfect roast potato should be crispy on the outside and soft yet dry inside.

6 LARGE GOLDEN WONDER POTATOES, PEELED AND ROUGHLY CUT INTO 3 OR 4

2 TBSP FLOUR, FOR DUSTING

RAPESEED OIL, FOR ROASTING

1 TSP CHOPPED ROSEMARY

10 SMALL SPRIGS OF ROSEMARY

5 GARLIC CLOVES, SLICED IN HALF

SEA SALT AND FRESHLY GROUND BLACK PEPPER

Preheat the oven to 210°C/fan 190°C/gas 7.

To cook the potatoes, place them in a steamer and cook for about 10 minutes. Remove and place in a colander or bowl and shake well so that the edges of the potatoes break slightly. Dust over the flour. Season with salt and freshly ground black pepper.

Heat some rapeseed oil in a roasting tin. Carefully add the floured potatoes, chopped rosemary and half the sprigs of rosemary and roast for about 20 minutes. Shake the roasting tin from time to time.

Add the garlic and reduce the heat to 200°C/fan 180°C/gas 6. Continue to roast for a further 15 to 20 minutes until the potatoes are crisp and golden.

Transfer to a warm serving dish and add a little more salt and the rest of the sprigs of rosemary.

Polenta and Parsley Chunky Parsnips

Serves 4

A great tip that I learned from an Italian chef who visited us is to soak peeled parsnips in half milk and half water to stop them turning brown. It really works but remember to rinse well and pat dry before cooking.

RAPESEED OIL

5 TO 6 LARGE PARSNIPS, PEELED AND SLICED INTO CHUNKS

4 TBSP FINE POLENTA (CORNMEAL)

SALT AND FRESHLY GROUND BLACK PEPPER

2 TSP CHOPPED PARSLEY, TO GARNISH

Preheat the oven to 210°C/fan 190°C/gas 7.

Heat some oil in a roasting tin.

Place the parsnips into a bowl and drizzle with some oil. Sprinkle the polenta over and toss very well.

Add the parsnip chunks to the heated oil and season with salt and freshly ground black pepper.

Roast for about 20 to 25 minutes until crisp and cooked.

Spoon the parsnips into a serving bowl, sprinkle the parsley over and keep warm until required.

CAULIFLOWER CHEESE BAKE

Serves 4

I often sprinkle toasted nuts or seed mix on top of this, and I sometimes use broccoli with the cauliflower florets, which gives great colour.

MELTED BUTTER, FOR BRUSHING

1 MEDIUM CAULIFLOWER, CUT INTO FLORETS

FOR THE SAUCE

4 TBSP BUTTER

2 TSP HAZELNUT OIL

2 ANCHOVIES, DRAINED AND VERY FINELY CHOPPED

4 TBSP PLAIN FLOUR

500ML MILK

SALT AND FRESHLY GROUND BLACK PEPPER

1 TSP WHOLEGRAIN MUSTARD

60G GRATED LOCAL MATURE CHEDDAR CHEESE

2 TBSP FLAKED ALMONDS, TO GARNISH

1 TBSP CHOPPED CHIVES

Preheat the oven to 210°C/fan 190°C/gas 7. Brush a gratin dish with a little melted butter.

Place the cauliflower florets in a steamer and cook for 15 to 18 minutes depending on the size.

Meanwhile, to make the sauce, place the butter, hazelnut oil, anchovies, plain flour, milk, salt and freshly ground black pepper into a saucepan over a medium heat. Whisk while it heats up and a thick sauce forms.

When the cauliflower is done, place the cooked florets into the prepared gratin dish ready for the sauce.

Add the mustard and three-quarters of the grated cheese to the sauce and simmer for 1 minute, whisking all the time. Pour the sauce over the cauliflower florets and sprinkle the rest of the grated cheese on top. Place in the oven to brown for about 5 to 6 minutes, but keep an eye on it.

Sprinkle over the almonds and chopped chives when ready to serve.

HONEY, RED WINE AND JUNIPER RED CABBAGE

Serves 4

Red cabbage is very durable, surviving heavy frosts through the winter. What's wonderful about this robust vegetable is its ability to take flavour, working well with Mediterranean and Asian influences.

2 TBSP BUTTER

2 RED ONIONS, SLICED

600G RED CABBAGE, SHREDDED

1 RED APPLE, SLICED INTO THIN WEDGES

1 TSP JUNIPER BERRIES, CRUSHED

1½ TBSP HONEY

1 TBSP BALSAMIC VINEGAR

100ML RED WINE

ABOUT 50ML WATER

SALT AND FRESHLY GROUND BLACK PEPPER

Heat the butter in a large saucepan, add the red onions and sauté for about 5 minutes.

Add the red cabbage, apple, juniper berries, honey, balsamic vinegar and red wine. Add a little water. Cover with a piece of parchment paper – this will create steam and help the vegetables to cook quicker.

Bring to the boil, reduce the heat and simmer for about 40 minutes, stirring from time to time.

Check the seasoning, adding salt and freshly ground black pepper. You may need to add a little more honey to taste.

There's something very special about home-grown produce —apart from doing the picking yourself, there's the achievement of growing them, the fresh flavours and, of course, the health benefits.

Purple Sprouting Broccoli with Wild Garlic Sauce

Serves 4

The purple sprouting broccoli and wild garlic season is just too short. They both have their own distinctive and delicate flavours so I never want to complicate them – this is simplicity at its best!

300G PURPLE SPROUTING BROCCOLI, TRIMMED AND OLDER LEAVES REMOVED

75G BUTTER

GOOD HANDFUL WILD GARLIC (ABOUT 30G), WASHED AND CHOPPED

½ LEMON, JUICE AND ZEST

SALT AND FRESHLY GROUND BLACK PEPPER

To cook the broccoli, place in a large saucepan of rapidly boiling, salted water. Cook until just al dente (to the bite) – this should take about 3 minutes. Drain and keep warm.

Heat the butter in a frying pan over a medium to high heat. Add the chopped wild garlic and sauté for 1 minute. Stir in the lemon juice and zest and season with salt and freshly ground black pepper.

Place the broccoli on a shallow serving platter, spoon over the garlic sauce and serve immediately.

Pan-fried Rainbow Chard with Garlic and Blue Cheese

Serves 4

There's something quite cheery about rainbow chard in the garden – those rubies, oranges, pinks and yellows look so impressive. It's a beautiful veg to accompany any main course.

RAPESEED OIL, FOR SAUTÉING

4 SMOKED BACON RASHERS, CUT INTO LARDONS

4 SHALLOTS, THINLY SLICED

3 GARLIC CLOVES, FINELY CHOPPED

1 TBSP CHOPPED CHIVES

12 LARGE CHARD LEAVES AND STEMS, TRIMMED AND ROUGHLY SHREDDED

1 TSP CELERY SEEDS

SALT AND FRESHLY GROUND BLACK PEPPER

2 TBSP CRUMBLED LOCAL ARTISAN BLUE CHEESE, FOR THE TOP

Heat a little oil in a large frying pan over a medium heat. Add the bacon lardons, sauté until crispy and set aside on a clean plate.

Add a little more oil followed by the shallots and sauté for 3 to 4 minutes until softened but not browned. Add the garlic and cook for 1 minute.

Stir in the bacon lardons, chopped chives, chard and celery seeds and toss well in the hot pan until the chard has wilted. Check the seasoning, adding a little salt and some freshly ground black pepper as needed.

To serve, transfer to a serving bowl and crumble a little blue cheese over the top.

Beetroot and Prosciutto Salad with Orange Dressing

Serves 4

There are many types of beetroot, the most common being the red, but I'm particularly keen on the golden and striped beetroot which look amazing roasted. I always have an abundance of the red beetroot so I roast and then freeze them to have on hand to make deliciously earthy soups.

EXTRA VIRGIN OLIVE OIL, FOR FRYING

100G PROSCIUTTO DI PARMA

100G FRENCH BEANS, SLICED DIAGONALLY INTO THIRDS

FOR THE DRESSING

½ RED CHILLI, FINELY CHOPPED

60ML EXTRA VIRGIN OLIVE OIL

1 TSP DIJON MUSTARD

1 ORANGE, JUICE AND ZEST

PINCH OF SUGAR

SALT AND FRESHLY GROUND BLACK PEPPER

GENEROUS BUNCH OF ROCKET OR YOUR FAVOURITE LETTUCE AND SPINACH LEAVES, WASHED AND TRIMMED

2 BEETROOT, STEAMED AND THINLY SLICED

2 TBSP TOASTED HAZELNUTS, ROUGHLY CHOPPED, TO GARNISH

Heat a little oil in a large frying pan over a medium heat and fry off the strips of prosciutto di Parma until crispy. Set aside on a clean plate.

Bring a saucepan of water to the boil and blanch the French beans for 3 minutes until slightly tender. Drain and refresh by placing in cold water.

To prepare the dressing, whisk together the chilli, oil, mustard and orange juice and zest. Add a pinch of sugar to taste and season with salt and freshly ground black pepper.

To assemble the salad, place the rocket leaves on a large platter and arrange the beetroot on top. Sprinkle the beans in between. Spoon some of the dressing over and pour the rest into a small jug to serve on the side. Lightly break up the crispy prosciutto di Parma and arrange on top. Sprinkle over the toasted hazelnuts.

Mint, Artichoke and Broad Bean Salad with Herb Dressing

Serves 4

Fantastic if you have artichokes in your garden but, of course, this recipe is lovely with canned ones too.

FOR THE DRESSING

2 LEMONS, ZEST AND JUICE

100ML RAPESEED OIL

2 TSP CASTER SUGAR

1 TBSP CHOPPED DILL

½ TSP PAPRIKA

SALT AND FRESHLY GROUND BLACK PEPPER

200G BROAD BEANS

100G YOUR FAVOURITE GARDEN LETTUCE LEAVES, WASHED

1 CUCUMBER, SLICED INTO RIBBONS

600G ARTICHOKE HEARTS IN OIL OR BRINE (TINNED OR IN A JAR), DRAINED

10 SMALL SPRIGS OF MINT, TO GARNISH

To make the dressing, place all the ingredients in a jar. Put the lid on tightly and shake well.

Blanch the broad beans in boiling water for 3 minutes then refresh in cold water, drain and remove the outer skins.

Place the lettuce leaves on a pretty serving platter.

To prepare the salad, place a layer of the broad beans around the outer edge of the plate, then a layer of cucumber ribbons inside and, finally, pile the artichoke hearts in the centre.

Spoon over some of the dressing, sprinkle the mint sprigs over the top and serve.

Chargrilled Courgette Salad with Crumbled Black Pudding and Chilli Sauce

Serves 4

I'm a great lover of salads in the winter months but they have to be warm, with a hot dressing poured over. If you don't fancy black pudding, try a local goat's cheese in this recipe.

FOR THE SAUCE

RAPESEED OIL

$1\frac{1}{2}$ RED CHILLIES, FINELY CHOPPED

2 LARGE TOMATOES, DESEEDED AND DICED

4 TBSP CASTER SUGAR

1 TBSP WHITE WINE VINEGAR

50ML WATER

SALT AND FRESHLY GROUND BLACK PEPPER

3 LARGE COURGETTES, SLICED ON THE DIAGONAL

3 TBSP POLENTA (CORNMEAL)

10 SMALL SPRIGS OF DILL, PLUS EXTRA TO GARNISH

100G GOOD QUALITY BLACK PUDDING, COOKED AND ROUGHLY CRUMBLED

To make the sauce, heat a little oil in a small saucepan over a medium heat. Add the chilli, tomato and sugar and simmer for about 4 minutes before adding the white wine vinegar and water. Season with salt and freshly ground black pepper. The sauce should taste slightly sweet. Set aside.

To cook the courgettes, dust them with polenta. Heat some more oil in a large chargrill pan over a medium heat and add the courgettes. Cook until golden, then set aside on kitchen paper to drain.

Assemble the salad by arranging the courgette slices on a serving platter and sprinkling over the dill sprigs. Spoon over the chilli sauce and crumble over the black pudding. Garnish with some more sprigs of dill and serve immediately.

When I first established our raised beds, I didn't realise or even dream that we would have a garden that would produce so much —and it is so satisfying.

Mangetout, Wicklow Blue Cheese and Borage Flower Salad with Strawberry Dressing

Serves 4

In the summer, try this dressing with vanilla ice cream but, hot tip: omit the oil!

FOR THE DRESSING

20 MEDIUM STRAWBERRIES, HULLED

3 BASIL LEAVES

1½ TBSP CASTER SUGAR

2 TBSP BALSAMIC VINEGAR

100ML EXTRA VIRGIN OLIVE OIL

SALT AND FRESHLY GROUND BLACK PEPPER

250G MANGETOUT OR SUGAR SNAP PEAS

GENEROUS HANDFUL BABY SPINACH LEAVES, TRIMMED

100G WICKLOW BLUE CHEESE, ROUGHLY DICED

BORAGE FLOWERS AND CHIVES, TO GARNISH

To make the dressing, place the strawberries into a blender, add the basil leaves and sugar and blend until puréed. Stir in the balsamic vinegar and oil and blend again. Check the seasoning, adding a little salt and freshly ground black pepper if required.

Bring a saucepan of water to the boil and blanch the mangetout or sugar snaps for 3 minutes until slightly tender. Drain and refresh by placing in cold water.

To assemble the salad, place the mangetout and spinach in a shallow bowl, drizzle with a little dressing and toss. Sprinkle over the cheese and spoon over some of the strawberry dressing.

Arrange the borage flowers and chives on top. Serve the extra dressing in a small jug on the side.

Shallot and Pear Tarte Tatin

Serves 4

Pears and shallots work so well together. Try them in salads too – add in a salty cheese such as goat's cheese or feta and you'll have a wonderful balance of flavours. You could also use this recipe to make individual tarts, which would be a lovely and interesting starter.

RAPESEED OIL, FOR SAUTÉING

6 SHALLOTS, FINELY SLICED

4 LARGE, FIRM PEARS, PEELED AND SLICED INTO WEDGES

1 LEMON, JUICE AND ZEST

50G SOFTENED BUTTER

4 TBSP CASTER SUGAR

6 SMALL SPRIGS OF THYME

SALT AND FRESHLY GROUND BLACK PEPPER

150G READY-TO-ROLL ALL-BUTTER PUFF PASTRY

EGG WASH, TO GLAZE

SMALL THYME SPRIGS, TO DECORATE

Heat a little oil in a saucepan over a medium heat and add the sliced shallots. Sauté for about 4 minutes until they are softened but not browned.

Place the pears in a medium-sized bowl and pour over the lemon juice and a little water to keep them from browning.

Preheat the oven to 200°C/fan 180°C/gas 6. Line the base of a 20cm springform tin with parchment paper.

Heat the butter and sugar in a small saucepan over a medium heat until melted and very lightly golden. Pour into the base of the springform tin. Neatly arrange the pears, lemon zest and thyme on top. Spoon the shallots over the pears and season with salt and freshly ground black pepper.

Roll the pastry out to just larger than the base of the tin. Carefully place over the pears, tucking in the edges.

Brush egg wash over the top and bake for about 20 to 25 minutes until golden and well risen.

Leave in the tin for at least 10 minutes to cool and set. Unclip the springform tin and flip the tarte tatin over onto a serving platter, so the pears are facing up.

Sprinkle over the thyme and enjoy.

Individual Tomato and Basil Summer Puddings

Makes 4

If you are looking for something tasty and different, this recipe will tick that box! I've always loved sweet summer pudding and was sure that a savoury one would be great. I tried this one day and it worked out excellently. The filling is a little like a gazpacho.

FOR THE FILLING

500G RIPE TOMATOES, DICED

3 TBSP RED WINE VINEGAR

1 TSP SUGAR

1 LEMON, JUICE ONLY

100ML EXTRA VIRGIN OLIVE OIL

6 BASIL LEAVES, TORN

2 TSP CHERVIL, FINELY CHOPPED

1 GARLIC CLOVE, FINELY CHOPPED

1 RED PEPPER, FINELY DICED

4 SPRING ONIONS, FINELY DICED

½ CUCUMBER, DESEEDED AND FINELY DICED

SALT AND FRESHLY GROUND BLACK PEPPER

EXTRA VIRGIN OLIVE OIL, FOR BRUSHING

12 SLICES STALE WHITE BREAD

SPRIGS OF BASIL, TO GARNISH

To make the filling, combine all the ingredients and season well. Leave in the fridge for 5 hours.

Brush 4 x 140ml ramekins or moulds with oil. Using a cutter the same size as the base, cut out 4 discs of bread. Brush the sides of the discs with oil and press one into each ramekin or mould. Cut out wedge-shaped pieces of bread to line the sides of the ramekins or moulds and press inside, leaving enough extra bread over the rim to fold over. Ensure that there are no gaps.

Spoon the tomato mixture into each ramekin or mould. Pack the mixture in, fold over the bread and press down firmly. You should have a little mixture left. Cover the puddings with clingfilm and place on a tray to catch any drips.

Place a weight (such as a tin of tuna) on each ramekin or mould, place a board on top and chill overnight.

To serve, bring the puddings to room temperature. Remove the clingfilm. Use a sharp knife to loosen the pudding and then invert each one onto a plate, giving it a gentle shake out of the ramekin or mould.

Spoon some of the leftover tomato mix around the plates, garnish with rocket leaves and sprigs of basil and serve immediately.

HERBS & FRUIT

Accompaniments and Preserves

One of the first jobs I undertook when I returned to the family home and business was to develop a herb and soft fruit garden. I've always admired Victorian-style gardens with box hedging, so that was my inspiration. Conveniently located between our cookery school and our farmhouse B&B, the garden supplies a wonderful crop of herbs, ranging from pineapple sage, purple sage, lemon verbena, Moroccan mint, eau de cologne mint, bronze fennel, chervil, English mace and salad burnet to the good old favourites like lavender, rosemary, thyme, chives, oregano and bay. I freeze chopped herbs in ice-cube trays or small bags when there is a glut. I can then pop them into soups and casseroles as I need them. I also make thyme- and rosemary-infused oils so that I can use them during the winter months. Herbal flowers are fabulous for decorating both sweet and savoury dishes and I just love purple chive flowers in salad. Camomile flowers make their way to my tisane, combined with a little honey and orange, and we use those gorgeous rosemary flowers to garnish lamb or even brighten chocolate tarts. Keeping the herbs company in the garden is a great array of fruits, from pears (that never seem to ripen!) to jostaberries, loganberries, gooseberries, blackcurrants, redcurrants, strawberries and raspberries, and nearby are the rhubarb plot and the old orchard. So we are never short of ingredients for the delicious jams and preserves my family loves to make!

How to ...
Plant a Micro Herb Garden

How about planting a micro herb patch on your window ledge? Growing herbs in jars is so rewarding.

To plant seeds

1   Put pebbles in a jar and fill with organic soil to just below the mouths.

2   Sprinkle in some seeds (about 5) and lightly cover with a little organic soil.

3   Water carefully, cover with a piece of clingfilm and leave in a warm sunny place.

4   After 3 days remove the wrap and water again. You'll need to lightly water about every 2 to 3 days.

5   Plant as many as you like, line them up along the window ledge and, when the herbs are ready, just cut what you need and they will grow again!

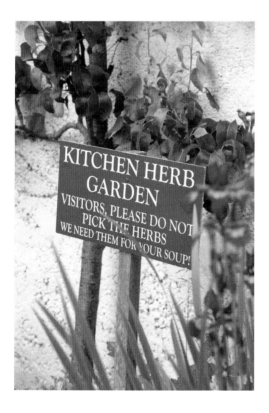

KITCHEN HERB
GARDEN
VISITORS, PLEASE DO NOT
PICK THE HERBS
WE NEED THEM FOR YOUR SOUP!

HERB SYRUPS

Makes about 350ml

Having flavoured stock syrups in the fridge is very useful. You can use them as cordials, over ice cream, with sparkling water, over a fruit salad, in a glass of Prosecco, in sauces or in baking.

FOR THE BASIC STOCK SYRUP

200G CASTER SUGAR

350ML WATER

FOR FLAVOURING
CHOOSE ONE OF THE FOLLOWING

4 LARGE, WASHED SPRIGS OF ROSEMARY

OR

1 WASHED, BRUISED LEMONGRASS STALK

OR

10 ORGANIC ROSE PETALS

OR

3 WASHED SWEET GERANIUM LEAVES (THIS CAN BE FAIRLY STRONG)

To make the basic stock syrup, add the sugar to a medium saucepan, pour over the water and bring to the boil. Reduce the heat and simmer for about 6 minutes until a light syrup forms.

Add the flavouring of your choice while the syrup is still hot and leave to cool completely so it can infuse. Then pour the syrup through a sieve into a jug or sterilised jar (see p. 133) and seal. Syrups will keep in the fridge for up to 3 weeks.

CHOCOLATE MINT LIQUEUR

Makes about 700ml

Confession time: I am a little fond of a) chocolate, b) a liqueur every now and again and c) mint, so I can't go wrong with this one!

250ML CREAM

10 LARGE SPRIGS OF MINT

5 TBSP CHOCOLATE SYRUP

397G CONDENSED MILK

180ML WHISKEY

½ TSP ALMOND EXTRACT

½ TSP VANILLA EXTRACT

To make the liqueur, warm the cream and mint in a medium saucepan to scalding point (when little bubbles start to form at the edges) then leave to cool. Pour the infused cream through a sieve, using a spoon to push the oils from the mint into the cream before removing the sprigs.

Gently whisk in the chocolate syrup, condensed milk, whiskey, almond extract and vanilla with the cream. Using a funnel, pour into a sterilised bottle (see p. 133). Store in the fridge – it will keep for 3 to 4 weeks. Serve over ice for a refreshing drink.

CATHERINE'S FAVOURITE PESTO

Makes about 400g

This is more of the Italian influence in our Wicklow family! There are a few items that are always in my fridge and one of them is my homemade pesto.

40G BASIL LEAVES

30G ROCKET LEAVES

100G HAZELNUTS, SKINS REMOVED AND LIGHTLY TOASTED

30G PECORINO

30G PARMESAN, GRATED

2 GARLIC CLOVES, ROUGHLY SLICED

150ML EXTRA VIRGIN OLIVE OIL, PLUS EXTRA TO COVER

SALT AND FRESHLY GROUND BLACK PEPPER

To make the pesto, place the basil, rocket leaves, hazelnuts, pecorino, Parmesan and garlic into a food processor. Pulse a few times and then, with the motor running, slowly add the extra virgin olive oil. Check the consistency: it should be thick yet able to drop off a spoon, so adjust the oil as needed. Check the seasoning, adding a little salt and freshly ground black pepper if required.

Spoon into a clean jar, pour a little extra virgin olive oil over the top, seal and place in the fridge, where it will keep for about 2 weeks.

HERB SALTS

Makes 2 x 100g jars

Having prepared flavoured salts in the kitchen is so practical and they are also a great little thank-you gift!

FOR THE ROSEMARY AND LEMON SALT

100G GOOD QUALITY SEA SALT

2 TSP CHOPPED ROSEMARY

1 LEMON, ZEST ONLY

FOR THE THYME AND CHILLI SALT

100G GOOD QUALITY SEA SALT

3 TSP CHOPPED THYME

2 TSP DRIED CHILLI FLAKES

2 JARS WITH TIGHT-FITTING LIDS

2 RIBBONS/STRINGS AND LABELS

In the first jar, place all the ingredients for the rosemary and lemon salt. In the second jar, place all the ingredients for the thyme and chilli salt. Seal both jars tightly and shake well. Label the jars and tie ribbons or string around them.

How to ...
MAKE GREAT JAM

To say I grew up with ladies who loved to make jam is an understatement. My mother and grandmother busied themselves throughout the summer and autumn as the frenzy of jam making took hold.

I've learned many things about jam making from my experiences over the years, so here are my top tips:

1 **NEVER** make large quantities in one pot, as it takes too long for the jam to come to the boil and the setting-point isn't always accurately reached.

2 The sugar should be **FULLY DISSOLVED** before you start boiling the fruit.

3 Always **STERILISE** your jars (see p. 133).

4 Add the cooked jam to **WARM** jars.

5 Use a **WIDE-NECKED** funnel – or, better still, a special jam funnel – when pouring the jam into the jars: it's far less messy!

6 Keep the jams in a **COOL, DARK** place and, once opened, keep them in the fridge.

STRAWBERRY AND BALSAMIC JAM

Makes about 1kg

The addition of the balsamic vinegar was a tip shared with me by a good friend. And it works! It enhances the sweetness of the strawberries and adds a lovely mellowness to the jam.

600G STRAWBERRIES, WASHED, HULLED AND SLICED IN HALF

600G JAM SUGAR

4 TBSP WATER

2 TBSP BALSAMIC VINEGAR

1 VANILLA POD, SEEDS SCRAPED OUT

1/2 LEMON, JUICE AND ZEST

1 TSP BUTTER

Place the strawberries in a large saucepan and crush gently. Then add in the jam sugar, water, balsamic vinegar, vanilla seeds and pod, as well as the lemon juice and zest. Stir over a gentle heat until the sugar has dissolved. Then bring to a rolling boil over a high heat and continue to boil until the setting point is reached (105°C). This can take up to 30 minutes, but check every 10 minutes. If you do not have a jam thermometer, place a saucer in the freezer to chill. To check manually, place a tablespoon of jam onto the chilled saucer, return to the fridge to cool for a minute and then push through it with your finger: if it wrinkles and the two halves remain separate, then it has reached setting point. Once this has been reached, stir in the butter and boil hard again for 1 minute.

Leave the jam to cool just slightly, then remove the vanilla pod and ladle into sterilised jars (see p. 133) through a funnel. Seal, label and store in a dark, cool place.

APPLE JELLY

Makes about 1.5kg

Our orchard here at Ballyknocken, planted by my grandparents, is a fantastic producer. I normally use crab apples in this recipe but if they're unavailable I use the smallest Bramleys. To strain the jelly, I learned a great trick from my mother. I turn a chair (not my best antique) upside down on another chair. Then I tack or nail (depending on the quantity and weight of the apple mix) a corner of a piece muslin to each of the 4 legs. I place a bowl underneath the muslin on the upside-down seat of the chair. Then I fill the muslin with the apple mix and leave it to drip overnight. It works like a dream every time!

1.5KG BRAMLEY APPLES, DICED (LEAVE THE PEEL ON)

2 LEMONS, JUICE ONLY

1 LITRE WATER

900G JAM SUGAR

3 TBSP PORT

To start making the jelly, place the diced apples and lemon juice into a saucepan with the water. Bring to the boil and simmer until the apple is soft and pulpy. Remove from the heat.

Have a sterilised jelly bag or muslin cloth ready and empty the contents of the pan into it. Leave to drip overnight into a bowl.

The next day, measure the juice – you should have about 1.2 litres. For every 650ml you will need to use 450g jam sugar.

Place the juice in a saucepan over a medium heat and bring to the boil. Add the sugar just as it comes to the boil and stir until the sugar is dissolved. Increase the heat and boil rapidly for about 20 minutes, stirring from time to time until the setting point is reached (105°C). Add the port and boil again. Check the setting point every 10 minutes but it may take up to half an hour.

If you don't have a jam thermometer, place a saucer in the freezer to chill. Place a tablespoon of jelly onto it, leave it for a minute in the fridge and then push through it with your finger. If it wrinkles and separates then it has reached setting point.

Skim the jelly. Leave to cool just slightly and ladle into sterilised jars (see p. 133) through a funnel. Seal, label and store in a cool place.

Ballyknocken's Famous Rhubarb and Ginger Jam

Makes about 2kg

This is my signature jam. I like the bite of the ginger, and many international visitors to our B&B have never seen or tasted rhubarb so it's always a great talking point!

1.3KG RHUBARB, WASHED, TRIMMED AND CUT INTO 4CM PIECES

4 TBSP WATER

2 TSP GROUND GINGER

1 LEMON, JUICE ONLY

1.3KG JAM SUGAR

Place the rhubarb, water, ginger and lemon juice into a saucepan. Bring to the boil and simmer gently for 10 minutes. Reduce the heat and add the jam sugar, stirring until it has all dissolved. Bring back to the boil and continue at a rolling boil for 10 to 15 minutes. During this time, skim off any froth that rises to the surface and place a saucer in the freezer.

Remove the saucepan from the heat and put a small amount of the jam onto the chilled saucer.

Return it to the fridge and, when cooled, run your finger through the centre of the jam. If the surface wrinkles and the two halves remain separate, then the jam has reached setting point. If not, put another saucer in the freezer and put the saucepan back on the heat for five minutes. Repeat the test until the setting point is reached (105°C).

Pour the jam into warm sterilised jars (see p. 133) and seal immediately. Allow to cool.

Store in a cool, dark place.

Cinnamon Pear Preserve

Makes about 1kg

Wicklow Blue from our local cheesemaker, John Hempenstal, makes a great combination with this oh-so-tasty pear preserve. The best thing is that unripe pears are needed for this recipe and I always have plenty of those in my garden. Still waiting on a blistering summer here in Wicklow!

500G CASTER SUGAR

150ML WATER

2 LEMONS, SLICED

1 CINNAMON STICK

SCANT PINCH OF NUTMEG

1/2 TSP FENNEL SEEDS

3 SMALL DRIED BAY LEAVES

7 LARGE, SLIGHTLY UNRIPE PEARS, PEELED, CORED AND SLICED INTO THIN WEDGES

Place the sugar, water, lemon slices, cinnamon stick, nutmeg, fennel seeds and bay leaves into a saucepan over a medium heat and simmer, carefully stirring until the sugar dissolves and a syrup forms.

Add the pear wedges and increase the heat slightly. Simmer gently until a thick syrup forms – this should take about 12 to 15 minutes. Stir from time to time.

Carefully spoon the preserve into sterilised jars (see p. 133), seal and label. Store the jars in a cool dark place until you are ready to use. Once open, keep in the fridge.

Plum and Red Onion Chutney

Makes about 1kg

We are all big fans of plums here and in the early autumn our orchard is laden with them. We make a feast of plummy goodies – they appear in compotes, jams, tray bakes, casseroles and in a lovely spicy plum sauce that I like as a treat over pannacotta. But this chutney is one of my favourites.

600G PLUMS, HALVED, STONED AND CHOPPED

1 COOKING APPLE, PEELED, CORED AND CHOPPED

2 RED ONIONS, FINELY CHOPPED

2 TBSP GRATED FRESH GINGER

2 SPRIGS OF ROSEMARY, FINELY CHOPPED

1 TSP SALT

1/2 TSP CHILLI FLAKES

500G SOFT BROWN SUGAR

350ML CIDER VINEGAR

Combine all the ingredients in a large, heavy-based saucepan and bring to the boil. Simmer uncovered over a very low heat, stirring occasionally with a wooden spoon. Continue to cook for 25 minutes, giving it a stir every 5 minutes, until the chutney is thick and syrupy.

Pour into sterilised jars (see p. 133), seal and label. Store in a cool place. Once opened, keep in the fridge.

MARSALA PEAR RELISH

Makes about 800g

The delicious flavours in this relish work extremely well with spicy curries and cheeseboards.

1 COOKING APPLE, PEELED, CORED AND CHOPPED

1 RED ONION, FINELY CHOPPED

5 DRIED APRICOTS, HALVED AND CHOPPED

1 TBSP GRATED FRESH GINGER

1 TSP CHOPPED ROSEMARY

1 TSP SALT

200G CASTER SUGAR

4 TBSP MARSALA

180ML WHITE WINE VINEGAR

500G PEARS, PEELED, CORED AND CUT INTO 2CM DICE

Combine all the ingredients except the pears in a medium-sized heavy-based saucepan and bring to the boil.

Simmer uncovered over a low heat, stirring occasionally. Continue to cook for about 15 minutes, giving the relish a stir every 5 minutes, until the mixture is syrupy.

Add the diced pears and cook for a further 12 to 15 minutes, stirring occasionally.

Pour into sterilised jars (see p. 133) and seal. Store in a dark place.

ON THE SWEETER SIDE

Cakes and Desserts

Because I grew up in a B&B where meals were served to guests every night, delectable desserts were the norm, not just a treat. So I had big pastry-chef's shoes to fill when I took over from my mother here at Ballyknocken. Dessert is my last chance to impress at a meal, so I love to see our guests' contented faces after a great one! Some desserts are always crowd pleasers and meringue in any form is one of them. Also anything with chocolate and fruits like pears or berries tends to impress. I am also always on the lookout for ways to decorate and present desserts, as it's not only about the flavours but also about the looks. I keep caramel shards, which look great to finish off a dessert and can be made ahead of time, in an airtight container. Candied orange slices look lovely too, as do edible flowers like borage, pinks and even rose petals, but they must be pesticide free. Herbs like rosemary, pineapple sage and thyme all work very well with desserts and I always keep berry syrups in little squeezy bottles to give an interesting burst of colour and flavour.

Mary's Eve's Pudding with Lemon Verbena Cream

Serves 6

This pudding is one that my mum could whip up in a flash – and it was gone in a flash as well! It's still a popular autumnal dessert in our house. The earliest known version of this recipe dates back to 1823. My mum's recipe was handed down through the generations and I've added my own twist.

FOR THE FILLING

2 TBSP BUTTER

6 LARGE COOKING APPLES, PEELED AND SLICED

1 LEMON, JUICE ONLY

4 TBSP SUGAR (DEPENDING ON HOW SWEET YOU LIKE IT)

¼ TSP GROUND CINNAMON

1 LARGE MANGO, PEELED AND DICED

FOR THE TOPPING

100G BUTTER, SOFTENED

100G GOLDEN CASTER SUGAR

3 FREE-RANGE EGGS

200G PLAIN FLOUR

2 HEAPED TSP BAKING POWDER

100G RASPBERRIES

3 TBSP TOASTED FLAKED ALMONDS, TO DECORATE

FOR THE CREAM

150ML CREAM

6 LEMON VERBENA LEAVES, FINELY SHREDDED

4 TBSP ICING SUGAR

MEDIUM SPRIG OF LEMON VERBENA, TO DECORATE

Preheat the oven to 190°C/fan 170°C/gas 6. Brush a 20 x 25cm gratin dish with a little melted butter.

To make the filling, melt the butter in a medium saucepan, add the apples, lemon juice, sugar and cinnamon and simmer for 5 to 6 minutes. Remove from the heat, add the diced mango and spoon into the prepared gratin dish. Leave to cool.

To make the topping, cream the butter and sugar until pale and fluffy. Add the eggs, one at a time, mixing well after each addition. Fold in the flour, baking powder and raspberries.

Spoon the topping mixture over the apples and bake in the preheated oven for 30 to 35 minutes.

The pudding should be risen and golden. Carefully insert a skewer into the topping and it should come out clean, bearing in mind that you have soft raspberries in the mix. Sprinkle over the toasted flaked almonds.

For the cream, whisk the cream to soft-peak stage, then fold in the shredded lemon verbena and icing sugar.

To serve, scoop a generous portion of the warm pudding into a pretty serving bowl, add a good dollop of the cream on top and garnish with a sprig of lemon verbena in the centre

ELDERFLOWER FRITTERS

Serves 4

The wonderful thing about food is that we are always learning. I was given this recipe by lovely Austrian guests who stayed with us one summer. These fritters have a decidedly distinctive floral flavour and elderflowers are so abundant that there's every reason to make them.

1 FREE-RANGE EGG, SEPARATED

50G FLOUR

50ML MILK

50ML SPARKLING WATER

RAPESEED OIL, FOR FRYING

5 LARGE ELDERFLOWER HEADS, SNIPPED INTO MANAGEABLE FLORETS, LEAVING THE STEMS AS LONG AS POSSIBLE

ICING SUGAR, TO DUST

Mix the egg yolk, flour, milk and sparkling water in a medium bowl. Set aside for 15 minutes.

Whisk the egg white until stiff and fold it into the batter.

Heat some oil in a frying pan.

Dip the florets into the batter and then, using the stems as a handle, lift them into the hot oil. Snip off the stem with a kitchen scissors. Cook for about 1 minute on each side until golden and crispy.

Transfer onto kitchen paper to drain.

Place on a serving platter, dust with a little icing sugar and enjoy!

Chocolate Mousse Cake

Serves 8 to 10

All I can say is that this is a proven favourite among our resident guests at Ballyknocken Farmhouse. Many have asked for the recipe, so here it is! (For a taller chocolate mousse, use a springform tin rather than a flan tin and simply increase the quantity of cream – anything up to 700ml will work nicely.)

FOR THE BASE

15 DIGESTIVE BISCUITS, FINELY CRUSHED

50G GROUND ALMONDS

100G MELTED BUTTER, PLUS EXTRA FOR BRUSHING

FOR THE FILLING

350G DARK CHOCOLATE (70% COCOA SOLIDS), BROKEN INTO SMALL PIECES

2 TBSP GOLDEN SYRUP

1 TSP COFFEE ESSENCE (OR 2 TSP COFFEE GRANULES DISSOLVED IN 2 TBSP HOT WATER)

3/4 TSP GROUND CINNAMON

500ML DOUBLE CREAM

COCOA POWDER, TO DECORATE

TOASTED FLAKED ALMONDS, TO DECORATE THE SIDES

CHOCOLATE CURLS, TO DECORATE

Brush a 20cm loose-based deep flan tin or springform tin with butter. Line the base with parchment paper.

To make the base, combine the biscuits and ground almonds and add enough melted butter to bind (the amount needed will depend on the size of the biscuits). Spoon the biscuit mix into the base and flatten. Place in the fridge to set for 30 minutes.

To make the filling, heat the chocolate, golden syrup, coffee essence and ground cinnamon in a medium saucepan over a very low heat. When the chocolate has melted, remove from the heat and allow to cool.

Meanwhile, whip the cream to soft-peak stage. Fold the cooled chocolate mix into the whipped cream and pour over the biscuit base. Leave to set in the fridge for at least 5 hours.

To serve, unmould from the tin and slide onto a cake stand. Dust the top with cocoa powder. Carefully pat toasted flaked almonds onto the sides of the cake and dust the excess off the cake stand. When you're ready to serve, place the chocolate curls in the centre of the cake.

Very Berry Pannacotta Tart

Serves 8 to 12

This recipe really was an invention – we needed something to use up the fresh fruit from our garden. I love pannacotta and so we began to experiment. It's an impressive dessert to look at, yet it's light and fresh in flavour. You can make it with any other suitable fruits, such as grapes, mango, papaya, kiwi and so on.

20 Rich Tea biscuits, crushed

1 lemon, zest only

100g melted butter

FOR THE FILLING

5 leaves gelatine

150ml cold water, to soften the gelatine leaves

300ml cream

70g caster sugar

1 tsp vanilla extract

250g natural yoghurt

FOR THE TOPPING

100ml water

60ml caster sugar

2 gelatine leaves

150ml cold water, to soften the gelatine leaves

100g blueberries

100g raspberries

100g loganberries or any other berry of your choice

Line the base of a springform tin with parchment paper.

Place the crushed biscuits into a bowl and add the lemon zest. Pour in sufficient butter to form a soft base. Spoon the biscuit mix into the tin and flatten. Place in the fridge to set for 30 minutes.

To make the filling, first soak the gelatine leaves in the cold water. This will soften them and make them pliable.

Place the cream and sugar into a saucepan and stir. Warm the mixture to dissolve the sugar and then bring it just to boiling point. Remove the pot from the heat and add the vanilla extract.

Squeeze the excess water from the gelatine leaves and place them into the cream mixture. Whisk briefly to dissolve. Add the yoghurt and whisk until smooth, then pour over the biscuit base. Cover with clingfilm and chill in the fridge for at least 4 hours or until set.

To prepare the topping, combine the water and sugar in a small saucepan and heat on medium to high until a thin syrup forms.

Meanwhile, soak the gelatine leaves in the cold water until soft, then squeeze the excess water and add the leaves to the syrup. Stir well until dissolved. Leave to cool and set slightly.

Remove the tart from the fridge and arrange all the berries on top. Mix the lightly set gelatine syrup and carefully pour over the top. Leave to set for at least 3 hours or overnight.

Mini Strawberry and Lemon Éclairs

Makes 24 small-to-medium size

I loved baking sweet treats as a child and young teen. Making choux pastry was one of my favourites. I loved éclairs more than profiteroles because I could get more cream into them and more chocolate on top!

FOR THE CHOUX PASTRY

250ML COLD WATER

80G BUTTER

PINCH OF SUGAR

PINCH OF SALT

125G STRONG FLOUR

4 FREE-RANGE EGGS (ABOUT 240G), BEATEN

EGG WASH, TO GLAZE

FOR THE FILLING

150ML CREAM, WHIPPED TO SOFT-PEAK STAGE

4 TBSP ICING SUGAR

1/2 LEMON, FINELY ZESTED

6 TO 8 STRAWBERRIES, HULLED AND THINLY SLICED

FOR THE TOPPING

100G WHITE CHOCOLATE, MELTED

4 STRAWBERRIES, SLICED, TO DECORATE

EDIBLE FLOWERS, TO DECORATE

Preheat the oven to 210°C/fan 190°C/gas 6.

To make the pastry, first bring the water and butter to the boil in a medium saucepan. Add the sugar and salt. Remove from the heat. Sift the flour onto a piece of parchment paper and 'shoot' the flour into the water and butter.

Return the mixture to the heat and stir briskly with a wooden spoon until the mixture leaves the sides of the pan. Beat in a little egg at a time until shiny and smooth, using a wooden spoon first and then a whisk. Once most of the egg is incorporated, the pastry should be soft but retain its shape when piped.

Line 2 baking trays with parchment paper.

Spoon the choux pastry into a piping bag fitted with a 1 to 1.5cm plain or star nozzle and pipe 5cm strips onto the sheets, leaving sufficient space in between for them to rise. Brush the tops with a little egg wash.

Bake in the preheated oven for about 25 minutes, depending on size, until the outsides of the éclairs are dry, crisp and golden but the insides are still slightly soft. Turn off the oven, slice down one side of each éclair and return them to the oven for 5 minutes.

Remove from the oven and place on a cooling rack.

To make the filling, combine the whipped cream, icing sugar and lemon zest and spoon into a piping bag.

When the éclairs are cold, fill them with the cream. Arrange a few slices of strawberry on the edge of each one. For the topping, fill a disposable piping bag or ziplock bag with the melted chocolate. Snip the end and pipe along the top of each éclair.

To serve, place a strawberry slice and an edible flower on each one and enjoy!

'THE PERFECT FOOLS' – GOOSEBERRY AND ELDERFLOWER AND BLACKCURRANT AND ROSEMARY

Serves 4

As a child I was always given the job of picking the gooseberries – the plants are pretty thorny and over the years I've noticed that the clever summer birds decimate my blackcurrant patch (as much as I allow them!) but still leave the gooseberries for me. Is there some divine message there? Gooseberry fool is one of the best desserts in my world – thank goodness the season is short otherwise I'd be eating fool all summer and having to walk it off more than I do already!

FOR THE GOOSEBERRY FOOL

200G GOOSEBERRIES, WASHED, TOPPED AND TAILED

50G CASTER SUGAR

2 TBSP ELDERFLOWER CORDIAL

200ML DOUBLE CREAM

3 TBSP ICING SUGAR

FOR THE BLACKCURRANT FOOL

200G BLACKCURRANTS, WASHED, TOPPED AND TAILED

75G CASTER SUGAR

2 MEDIUM SPRIGS OF ROSEMARY

200ML DOUBLE CREAM

3 TBSP ICING SUGAR

4 SPRIGS OF MINT OR ROSEMARY, TO DECORATE

SHORTBREAD BISCUITS, TO SERVE

To make the gooseberry fool, combine the berries, sugar and cordial in a medium saucepan over a low heat and simmer for about 5 minutes. Remove from the heat and leave to cool completely.

Lightly whip the cream with the icing sugar until it reaches soft-peak stage.

Set aside 2 tbsp of the compote, then gently combine the rest with the cream so that it creates a marbling effect.

If serving the fools separately, neatly spoon the mix into small glasses, top with the reserved compote and leave to set in the fridge for an hour.

To make the blackcurrant fool, combine the berries, sugar and rosemary sprigs in a medium saucepan over a low heat and simmer for about 6 minutes until softened. Leave to cool, then remove the rosemary sprigs.

Lightly whip the cream and icing sugar to soft-peak stage. Set aside 2 tbsp of the compote and gently combine the cream with the rest of it to create a marbling effect.

If serving separately, neatly spoon into small glasses, top with some compote and leave in the fridge for an hour to set.

Alternatively, if serving the fools together, spoon some gooseberry fool into the base of a taller glass, followed by some of the gooseberry compote. Then top with some of the blackcurrant fool, topped with some of the compote.

To serve, place either a glass of each fool or the tall glass with both on a board or plate, decorate with mint or rosemary sprigs and serve with shortbread biscuits.

'To Die For' Lemon Meringue Pie

Serves 6 to 8

My mother was most definitely the queen of lemon meringue pie, to the point where we as children became quite the connoisseurs, recognising the good, the bad and the ugly of this wonderful dessert. I like my lemon meringue filling to be fairly sharp, as a contrast to the soft marshmallow topping, and you can't go wrong with serving lemon meringue to a crowd.

FOR THE PASTRY

MELTED BUTTER, FOR BRUSHING

200G PLAIN FLOUR, PLUS A LITTLE EXTRA FOR DUSTING

2 TBSP GROUND ALMONDS

150G CHILLED BUTTER, ROUGHLY DICED

1 FREE-RANGE EGG YOLK

1 TO 2 TBSP COLD WATER

EGG WASH, TO GLAZE

FOR THE FILLING

5 FREE-RANGE EGG YOLKS

250G CASTER SUGAR

50G BUTTER

5 LEMONS, ZEST OF 2 AND JUICE OF 5

3 TBSP CORNFLOUR

FOR THE MERINGUE TOPPING

5 FREE-RANGE EGG WHITES

250G CASTER SUGAR

2 TSP CORNFLOUR

Brush a deep loose-based 23cm flan tin with some melted butter. Dust with a little flour.

To make the pastry, place the flour, ground almonds and butter into a food processor and blend until the mixture looks like fine breadcrumbs. Pour in the egg yolk and pulse to form a soft pastry dough. Add a little cold water if needed.

Roll the pastry out between 2 pieces of clingfilm and then peel off the top piece. Turn over and carefully line the dusted flan tin with the pastry. Peel off the other piece of clingfilm. Place in the fridge for 30 minutes to rest.

Preheat the oven to 200°C/fan 180°C/gas 4. Place a piece of parchment paper over the pastry and pour in baking beans. Bake for about 20 minutes and then remove the baking beans and parchment paper. Brush the pastry with egg wash and bake again for about 10 minutes until golden. Set aside. Reduce the oven temperature to 180°C/fan 160°C/gas 4.

To make the filling, whisk the egg yolks and sugar together in a large saucepan over a medium heat. Whisking all the time, add the butter, then pour in the lemon zest and juice. Whisk in the cornflour and simmer until a thick sauce/filling develops. It is best to keeping whisking while the filling is thickening. Set aside.

To make the meringue topping, whisk the egg whites to soft-peak stage. Gradually add the sugar until a thick meringue develops. Fold in the cornflour.

Pour the lemon filling into the baked pastry case and spoon or pipe the meringue topping over, starting from the outer edge and working to the centre, ensuring that you make peaks. Transfer to the preheated oven for 18 to 20 minutes until golden and brown.

Cool on a rack then serve with a delicious farmhouse vanilla ice cream.

Prosecco, Lemon Balm and Blueberry Jellies

Serves 6 in small glasses

There is something so elegant and light about this over-eighteens fruit jelly – it's particularly suitable after a rich main course.

350ML Prosecco

4 TBSP SUGAR

3 LARGE SPRIGS LEMON BALM

4 LEAVES GELATINE

150ML COLD WATER, TO SOFTEN THE GELATINE

100G BLUEBERRIES, WASHED

6 SMALL SPRIGS OF LEMON BALM, TO DECORATE

Place 6 small glasses on a tray in the fridge to chill.

Heat 150ml of the Prosecco, the sugar and lemon balm sprigs in a medium saucepan over a medium heat until the sugar has melted. Remove the lemon balm sprigs.

Place the gelatine leaves in the cold water and leave to soften. Once softened, squeeze out the excess water, then add the leaves to the warm Prosecco and whisk well until melted. Pour into a jug and add the remaining 200ml Prosecco. Refrigerate and stir frequently until the mix just begins to set (about 1 hour) – this will stop the fruit from floating to the top.

Divide the blueberries between the 6 chilled glasses and pour over the partially set jelly mixture. Cover with clingfilm and place in the fridge overnight.

To serve, place a sprig of lemon balm on the edge of each glass and serve on a plate with a long teaspoon and some delicate Amaretti biscuits.

Blackberry and Rhubarb Upside-Down Cake

Serves 6 to 8

This cake was originally a pineapple and cherry upside-down cake which was made daily here at Ballyknocken for hungry hillwalking guests. Because of my love for all that my garden produces, I'm using delicious rhubarb here.

MELTED BUTTER, FOR BRUSHING

FLOUR, FOR DUSTING

12 RHUBARB STALKS, TRIMMED AND CUT IN 8CM LENGTHS

4 TBSP BROWN SUGAR

FOR THE TOPPING

60G BUTTER, SOFTENED

120G SOFT LIGHT BROWN SUGAR

200G BLACKBERRIES

¼ TSP GROUND CINNAMON

FOR THE CAKE

100G BUTTER, SOFTENED

80G GOLDEN CASTER SUGAR

1 TSP VANILLA EXTRACT

3 FREE-RANGE EGGS

200G PLAIN FLOUR, SIFTED

1½ TSP BAKING POWDER

DUSTING OF ICING SUGAR, TO DECORATE

Preheat the oven to 180°C/fan 160°C/gas 4. Line the base of a square 20cm baking tin with parchment paper. Brush the sides with melted butter and dust with a little flour.

Place the rhubarb pieces on a roasting tin, sprinkle over the 4 tbsp brown sugar and roast until just cooked and lightly caramelised.

For the topping, cream the butter and sugar until light and fluffy. Spoon into the base of the baking tin.

Arrange the roasted rhubarb lengths around the outer edge of the baking tin and pour over the juices from the roasting tin. Place the blackberries in the centre and sprinkle the ground cinnamon over the fruit.

To make the cake batter, cream the butter, sugar and vanilla extract until pale and fluffy. Add the eggs one at a time, mixing well after each addition. Fold in the flour and baking powder. Spread the cake batter over the arranged fruit and bake in the preheated oven for about 30 to 35 minutes until well risen, golden and cooked. Insert a skewer into the cake and check that it comes out clean, but be aware of the cooked fruit lower down.

Transfer to a cooling rack and leave to set in the tin for about 15 minutes. Then carefully slide a sharp, thin knife around the edge of the tin. Place a plate on top and quickly turn over. Remove the parchment paper.

Dust with icing sugar and serve warm with lots of whipped cream.

WICKLOW SUMMER PUDDING

Serves 6

I use any variety of berries in this pudding, depending on what there is to hand. I often have frozen berries – whenever I have a glut in the garden I freeze them, which is easy to do. Simply rinse the berries, then place on a parchment paper-lined tray and pop into the freezer for an hour until set. Then gather them into bags and freeze until needed.

800G MIXED BERRIES (E.G. 300G RASPBERRIES, 250G BLACKBERRIES AND 250G STRAWBERRIES)

You could also use blueberries, blackcurrants, redcurrants or loganberries

100G CASTER SUGAR

1 SMALL ORANGE, ZEST ONLY

2 TBSP ELDERFLOWER CORDIAL (OR SHERRY)

RAPESEED OIL, FOR BRUSHING

8 SLICES 2CM-THICK GOOD QUALITY WHITE BREAD, CRUSTS CUT OFF AND 6 OF THEM CUT INTO THIRDS

WHIPPED CREAM, TO SERVE

SMALL SWEET GERANIUM LEAVES, TO DECORATE

Place the berries into a large saucepan and add the sugar, orange zest and cordial or sherry. Warm gently – the fruit will loosen some juice. Remove from the heat.

Brush a 1.2 litre pudding bowl with oil and line with a double layer of clingfilm with a generous overhang.

Cut a disc of bread to fit the base of the pudding bowl and one to fit the top. Line the pudding bowl with the rest of the bread pieces, overlapping each one. Spoon the berries into the pudding bowl and fit the last round bread disc on the top as a lid.

Cover with the overhanging clingfilm and place on a tray. Place another tray over it with heavy weights, such as 2 cans of beans, on top. Leave in the fridge overnight to soak up all the berry juices.

To serve, open the clingfilm on top and slide a knife around the inside of the pudding bowl. Place a plate on top and quickly turn over. Gently shake to dislodge. Peel off the clingfilm.

Serve with whipped cream and decorate with a few sweet geranium leaves.

HARVEST TIMES

Breads and Baking

There has always a great smell of baking wafting through our farmhouse – it's a family tradition. If my mother and granny weren't baking for the B&B, they were baking for the ICA or for a friend's birthday or for my uncle who was coming over for tea and scones. The mammoth baking days were during the harvesting, when lots of local help arrived on the farm. Truckloads of sandwiches, cakes, buns and the likes were delivered out to the fields. I find baking rather therapeutic. It's my time to step back from the rush of daily life and take it slowly. And the bonus is that there is nothing quite like freshly made bakes and sweet treats just out of the oven. It's good for the soul, for sure!

Ballyknocken Soda Seed Bread

Makes 1 loaf

Every family has their own soda bread recipe that goes back generations. I have a number of them – my granny's traditional oval-shaped one, my mother's 'modernised' Pyrex-bowl version and my own one, shared here.

2 TBSP SOFT DARK-BROWN SUGAR

200G PLAIN FLOUR

200G WHOLEMEAL FLOUR

1¼ TSP BREAD SODA (BICARBONATE OF SODA)

3 TBSP TOASTED HAZELNUTS, CHOPPED

1 TBSP PUMPKIN SEEDS

2 TBSP TOASTED SESAME SEEDS

1 TBSP SUNFLOWER SEEDS

2 TBSP RAPESEED OIL

250ML BUTTERMILK

60ML COLD WATER (YOU MAY NEED A LITTLE MORE)

1 TSP PUMPKIN SEEDS AND 1 TSP SUNFLOWER SEEDS, TO DECORATE

Preheat the oven to 180°C/fan 160°C/gas 4. Line a 900g loaf tin with parchment paper.

Add the sugar and plain and wholemeal flours to a large mixing bowl. Sift in the bread soda and mix well. Add the hazelnuts, pumpkin seeds, sesame seeds and sunflower seeds and pour in the oil. Add the buttermilk and then add enough cold water to form a soft bread mix.

Pour into the lined loaf tin, sprinkle the extra seeds over the top and transfer to the oven for about 50 minutes.

To test that it is done, insert a clean skewer into the bread – if it comes out clean, it is cooked. Or tap the bread on the base – if it sounds hollow then it is cooked.

Transfer to a rack and leave to cool completely.

SODA FARLS

Makes 4

In the parlour room, which was the kitchen, we still have the original fireplace and Dad tells us that many soda farls were made on the griddle over the open fire. I can just imagine lots of laughter, warm, welcoming farls with dollops of raspberry jam and many cups of tea being enjoyed there.

400G PLAIN FLOUR, PLUS EXTRA FOR DUSTING

½ TSP SALT

1 TSP BREAD SODA (BICARBONATE OF SODA)

250ML BUTTERMILK

2 TBSP BUTTER, FOR THE GRIDDLE

Place the flour into a medium mixing bowl, add the salt and sift in the bread soda. Mix thoroughly. Make a well in the centre and pour in enough buttermilk to form a dough. Mix well. If the dough is too stiff, add a few tablespoons of water.

Dust a clean surface with flour. Place the dough on the floured surface and shape into a circle about 4cm high and 18cm in diameter. Slice into quarters with a sharp knife.

Heat a griddle pan or large frying pan over a medium to high heat and brush with a little butter. Place the soda farl quarters onto the pan and cook for about 5 to 6 minutes until golden on each side.

Serve with butter and homemade jam.

Mary's Brown Bread

Makes 1 round loaf

This is a 'fond memory' bread which my mother made very often – and in two minutes flat we'd demolish it! It's made in a Pyrex bowl.

225G PLAIN FLOUR

225G WHOLEMEAL FLOUR

1 TSP SALT

1 TSP BREAD SODA
(BICARBONATE OF SODA)

1 TBSP MOLASSES

40G BUTTER, MELTED
(ABOUT 2 TBSP), PLUS
EXTRA FOR BRUSHING

1 FREE-RANGE EGG,
BEATEN

380ML BUTTERMILK

Preheat the oven to 200°C/fan 180°C/gas 6. Brush a 900ml Pyrex bowl with melted butter.

Place the flours and salt into a large bowl. Sift in the bread soda and mix well. Put the molasses, melted butter, egg and buttermilk in a jug and whisk well. Add the buttermilk mixture to the dry ingredients and mix to form a soft dough.

Transfer to the prepared Pyrex bowl.

Bake in the preheated oven for 40 minutes. To check that the loaf is cooked, tap the base – it should sound hollow.

Transfer to a cooling rack. If you want a soft crust, cover with a damp tea towel.

LEMONADE, WHITE CHOCOLATE AND FRAUGHAN SCONES

Makes 12

We have had many Australian visitors to our cookery school over the years and they have shared this scone recipe with me. But I just had to add a little Irish twist to it – fraughans, which we forage for up in the forest. There is even a Fraughan Sunday – the last Sunday in July – when families traditionally go out to gather the berries. But be warned: fraughans are quite sour! If you can't get your hands on any, blueberries are a good alternative.

300G SELF-RAISING FLOUR, PLUS EXTRA FOR DUSTING

¾ TSP BAKING POWDER

4 TBSP WHITE CHOCOLATE DROPS OR CHIPS

3 TBSP FRAUGHANS OR BLUEBERRIES

100ML CREAM

150ML LEMONADE

EGG WASH, TO GLAZE

2 TBSP CASTER SUGAR, FOR THE TOP

Preheat the oven to 210°C/fan 190°C/gas 7. Line a baking tray with parchment paper.

Add the flour and baking powder to a medium mixing bowl. Spoon the chocolate and fraughans or blueberries into the flour. Pour in the cream and enough of the lemonade to form a soft scone dough.

Place the dough on a clean surface dusted with flour and pat out gently to about 3cm in thickness. Using a medium-sized cutter, cut out scones, glaze with egg wash and dip the tops into the sugar. Transfer the scones, sugar side up, to the baking tray and bake for about 15 to 17 minutes until golden and well risen. They won't hold a perfect scone shape because of the fraughans or blueberries in them, but that's ok.

Transfer to a cooling rack, then serve with butter, jam and cream. They are best enjoyed whilst fresh.

There is nothing quite like freshly made bakes and sweet treats just out of the oven. It's good for the soul, for sure.

Caramelised Onion and Leek Scones

Makes 12, depending on the size

These flavoursome scones will add that 'wow' to any meal from brunch to a dinner party, where they could accompany a soup. They're a great crowd pleaser, especially in our cookery school.

1 TBSP BUTTER

2 TBSP OLIVE OIL

2 MEDIUM ONIONS, FINELY CHOPPED

1/2 LARGE LEEK, FINELY SLICED

250G PLAIN FLOUR, PLUS EXTRA FOR ROLLING

2 TSP BAKING POWDER

1/2 TSP BREAD SODA (BICARBONATE OF SODA)

1/2 TSP SALT

1 TBSP SUGAR

60G CHILLED BUTTER, DICED

40G GRATED PARMESAN

120G NATURAL YOGHURT (YOU MAY NEED A LITTLE MORE DEPENDING ON THE THICKNESS)

EGG WASH, TO GLAZE

Preheat the oven to 220°C/fan 200°C/gas 6. Line a baking tray with parchment paper.

Heat the butter and olive oil in a frying pan and cook the onions and leek over a low heat, stirring from time to time, until softened but not browned. This will take about 7 to 8 minutes.

Transfer the cooked onion and leek to a small bowl, straining off the excess butter and oil in the process, and set aside.

Sift the flour, baking powder and bread soda into a large bowl. Add the salt and sugar. Using your fingers, rub the chilled butter into the flour until it resembles fine breadcrumbs. Stir the Parmesan, onions and leek into the flour mix. Carefully mix in the yoghurt to form a soft dough.

Transfer to a floured surface and knead lightly for a few seconds. Pat the dough out to about 2.5cm thick. Using a medium-sized cutter, cut out rounds and place on the baking tray. Brush the tops with egg wash and transfer to the preheated oven.

Bake for about 15 to 18 minutes, depending on the size, keeping an eye on them, until lightly golden and risen. Transfer to a cooling rack to cool.

OATY CHIVE BISCUITS

Makes about 24 to 30, depending on the size

You may have to seal these tightly and keep them out of sight, as they are very moreish with a few slices of good local cheese!

100G PLAIN FLOUR, PLUS EXTRA FOR DUSTING

100G WHOLEMEAL FLOUR

4 TBSP PORRIDGE OATS

½ TSP BREAD SODA (BICARBONATE OF SODA)

1 TSP CASTER SUGAR

½ TSP SALT

½ TSP PAPRIKA

60G BUTTER, DICED

1 TBSP FINELY CHOPPED CHIVES

½ TSP DIJON MUSTARD

1 LARGE FREE-RANGE EGG YOLK

2 TO 4 TBSP WATER

Preheat the oven to 180°C/fan 160°C/gas 4. Line 2 baking trays with parchment paper.

Place the plain flour, wholemeal flour and oats into a bowl. Sift in the bread soda. Spoon in the sugar, salt and paprika and stir well. Add the diced butter and rub together to form breadcrumbs. Add the chopped chives and mustard. Stir in the egg yolk and enough water to form a stiff dough.

Roll the dough out thinly on a floured surface. Cut out circles with a scone cutter and place on the lined trays.

Bake for 20 to 25 minutes until lightly browned. Transfer to a cooling rack and store in an airtight container until required.

Aunty Trina's Tea Brack

Makes a 900g loaf

My Aunty Trina, bless her, gave me this and it remains one of my much-loved recipes – a comforting slice served with a good cuppa is always uplifting! It's a tea brack but we like to add a few trinkets to the mix, wrapped in parchment and foil, as with a traditional barm brack. As kids, we enjoyed the fun of finding wrapped coins and rings (meaning wealth and marriage respectively). We omitted the older traditions of a pea (meaning no marriage that year) and a stick (an unhappy marriage), as there's no fun in that!

350ML COLD IRISH BREAKFAST TEA

540G SULTANAS

275G SUGAR

275G BUTTER, PLUS EXTRA FOR GREASING

400G SELF-RAISING FLOUR

1 TSP MIXED SPICE

2 TO 3 TBSP CHOPPED NUTS AND GLACÉ CHERRIES (OPTIONAL)

3 TO 4 BEATEN EGGS

Preheat the oven to 180°C/fan 160°C/gas 4. Line a 22.5cm square cake tin with greased parchment paper. Wrap trinkets such as coins and rings in parchment paper (as tightly and neatly as possible).

Put the tea, sultanas, sugar and butter into a saucepan and bring to the boil. Boil for 5 to 10 minutes. Remove from the heat and allow to cool.

Sift the flour and mixed spice into a large bowl. Add the nuts and cherries, if using.

When the boiled mixture has cooled, pour into the flour and mix well. Add the beaten eggs and mix well again. Pour into the prepared cake tin. Push the wrapped trinkets into the cake mixture (below the surface, so there is no trace of them when the cake is cooked).

Bake for approximately 1½ hours. After 30 minutes reduce the oven temperature to 160°C/fan 140°C/gas 3 for the remainder of the cooking time. Test with a skewer – if it comes out clean, the cake is ready.

CHURN IT UP

Milk and Cheese

My father and grandfather were dairy farmers, so we were spoilt growing up. We used to let the fresh unpasteurised milk settle and then skim the most delicious cream from the top of the milk buckets. Then we would make our own butter – that was some job. We had an antique churn and my brother and I had to take turns at turning the handle. No breaks were allowed on the butter-making shift! As we focused more on lamb farming in the past few decades, I decided to make use of the milking parlour by converting it into our cookery school.

How to ...
Make Yoghurt and Butter

We are lucky in Ireland to have such amazing milk. Our cows graze happily in the pastures and this results in fantastic dairy produce. In our cookery school, we give lessons in how to use this wonderful milk to make yoghurt and butter. Why not give it a try yourself?

Yoghurt

Yoghurt is fairly simple to make but takes time. You'll need a medium saucepan, thermometer, wide-mouthed Thermos and sieve.

Place 500ml milk in the saucepan with 1 tbsp sugar and heat to 85°C. Cool to 46°C and then add 3 tbsp of room-temperature natural plain yoghurt made with organic live cultures. Pour into the Thermos and leave for 7 hours.

At this point, the yoghurt should be thick and custard-like with a very slightly cheesy smell.

Strain through a sieve and then spoon into a clean jar. It will keep for about 4 days or so in the fridge. To flavour, add berry compotes, chopped nuts or flavoured stock syrup.

Butter

Making butter isn't all that difficult. You don't need a churn if you're making small quantities – an electric stand mixer will do the job.

Pour 800ml thick cream into the bowl of a mixer and whisk on medium speed until very thick. Change the whisk to the paddle attachment and beat at full power until the butter solids separate from the liquid, which is now buttermilk. Pour the buttermilk (which looks like cloudy water) off and keep in the fridge. It is great for baking and to use in curries.

To rinse the butter, pour about 200ml ice-cold water into the bowl and, using a spatula, work the water through the butter to get all the buttermilk out – it tends to lodge in pockets. Do this 3 or 4 times until the water is clear.

Now you can add a sprinkle of salt, shape it into a rectangular block, wrap in parchment and refrigerate.

THREE FLAVOURED BUTTERS

Using flavoured butters is such an easy way of adding more interest to dishes. I have a small box in the fridge with rolls of parchment-wrapped flavoured butters in it – just remember to label them, as chilli, lime and cumin butter on a warm fruit scone isn't that appetising! These flavoured butters will keep in the fridge for about 3 weeks; it's also possible to freeze them. Slice them with a warm knife and use them over steaks, chicken fillets or roast beef. Serve them with poached or steamed vegetables as well as in sauces and, don't forget, sweet butters are delicious with warm scones and tea bracks.

Each makes a 15cm roll

FOR SWEET ORANGE AND CINNAMON BREAKFAST BUTTER

120g unsalted butter, softened
1 orange, zest only
2 tbsp icing sugar
½ tsp ground cinnamon

FOR CELERY SEED AND BLACK OLIVE BUTTER

120g salted butter, softened
¼ tsp salt
2 tbsp celery seeds
12 black olives, finely diced
½ tsp paprika

FOR CHILLI, LIME AND CUMIN BUTTER

120g salted butter, softened
¼ tsp salt
1 red chilli, finely diced
2 limes, zest only
1 tsp ground cumin

For each recipe, mix the ingredients together in a small bowl. Lay a piece of parchment paper out. Spoon the flavoured butter onto the parchment in a 15cm long line. Using the parchment, roll it into a log shape. Twist both ends of the paper and place in the fridge to set.

When ready to use, slice.

THREE YOGHURT DRESSINGS

❖❖❖

HONEY AND GINGER YOGHURT DRESSING

Makes 180ml

Try this over a summery radish, strawberry and dill salad – it's the best!

2 tsp honey
2cm fresh ginger, grated
1 tbsp chopped chives
160g natural yoghurt
1 tsp rice vinegar
salt and freshly ground
black pepper

Combine all the ingredients in a small bowl and whisk well. Check the seasoning and add a little more salt and freshly ground black pepper if needed. Transfer to a jar until ready to use. It will keep in the fridge for a week or so.

TAHINI YOGHURT DRESSING

Makes 150ml

I serve this as a zesty dip with koftas or fish cakes.

100g natural yoghurt
1 tbsp tahini paste
½ lemon, zest and juice
salt and freshly ground
black pepper
1 tbsp toasted sesame
seeds

Mix the yoghurt and tahini paste together very well before adding the lemon zest and juice. Check the seasoning, adding salt and freshly ground black pepper as needed. Stir in the toasted seeds. Transfer to a jar – it will keep in the fridge for about 5 days.

HONEY AND APPLE YOGHURT DRESSING

Makes 250ml

This is delicious with prawns, homemade goujons or over a fish salad.

200g natural yoghurt
1 tbsp honey
50ml apple cider or apple
juice
¼ tsp paprika
1 tbsp mixed fresh herbs,
such as parsley, thyme and
chives
salt and freshly ground
black pepper

Combine the yoghurt, honey and apple cider in a bowl and mix well. Add the paprika and stir again. Sprinkle in the herbs and check the seasoning, adding salt and freshly ground black pepper to taste. Leave for 3 to 4 hours for all the flavours to infuse before using. This will keep for about 4 days in the fridge.

Apricot and Lemon Balm Yoghurt Cake

Serves 8

Lemon balm grows so well in our herb garden here that it's quite difficult to stop it! It is wonderful for baking, for fruit compotes and even for flower arrangements, as its sweet lemon scent fills the rooms.

120ML OLIVE OIL

3 EGGS

190G CASTER SUGAR

1 LEMON, ZEST AND JUICE

300G NATURAL YOGHURT

320G SELF-RAISING FLOUR

8 DRIED APRICOT HALVES, FINELY CHOPPED

4 LARGE LEMON BALM LEAVES, FINELY CHOPPED

SPRIGS OF LEMON BALM, TO DECORATE

To make the cake, preheat the oven to 190°C/fan 170°C/gas 5. Line a 20cm deep loose-based cake tin with parchment paper.

Put the oil, eggs and sugar into a mixing bowl and whisk them well before adding the lemon zest and juice. Pour in the yoghurt and whisk again. Fold in the flour, chopped apricots and lemon balm.

Pour the batter into the prepared tin and bake for 25 to 30 minutes until golden or when a skewer is inserted and comes out clean. Transfer to a cooling rack and allow to cool in the tin.

Decorate with lemon balm sprigs on top when you are ready to serve.

A Celebratory Cheese Cake

Makes 1

These are all the rage at weddings and parties. They look stunning and who doesn't love farmhouse cheese? Depending on the number of guests, the tower can be as small or as large as you like.

4 OR 5 DIFFERENT SIZES TYPES OF CHEESE OF YOUR CHOICE (E.G. A BRIE, A MATURE CHEDDAR, A SMOKED CHEDDAR, A BLUE VEIN, A PORTER CHEESE, A FLAVOURED DILLISK CHEESE OR A GOAT'S CHEESE)

BLACKBERRIES OR RASPBERRIES, TO DECORATE

EDIBLE FLOWERS, SUCH AS VIOLAS AND BORAGE, TO DECORATE

10 TO 12 SMALL SWEET GERANIUM LEAVES, TO DECORATE

10 SMALL SPRIGS OF BAY

10 MEDIUM SPRIGS OF ROSEMARY, TO DECORATE

Place a thick, round wooden board on a table or large tray. Place the largest cheese on it and then the next largest on top of that and so on until the smallest cheese is on the top.

Arrange the blackberries or raspberries around the edges.

Add the flowers, leaves, sprigs of bay and rosemary around the entire cheese cake. Stand back and appreciate your creativity!

CHEESEBOARD ESSENTIALS

Makes 12

Cheese looks great served on wooden boards, slates or even a nice tray, but more important, of course, are the cheeses themselves – as well as the extras. I often add a good chutney which isn't too spicy, some slices of fresh fig, bay leaves and rosemary sprigs to garnish, toasted whole nuts, fruits such as chargrilled nectarines, melon or Marsala-roasted grapes, and even honey in the comb. But the candied walnuts and apple crisps below are two of my very favourite accompaniments and are sure to be a hit with your guests too! A cheeseboard is, in a sense, a meal, so serve it in abundance on a summer's day as a main dish with salads and charcuterie. For a simple board to suit all tastes, I'd suggest a mature Cheddar, a soft Brie and a blue and then add two of your own favourites, such as a lovely sheep's cheese and perhaps an earthy smoked cheese. When arranging boards, include enough cheese knives and labels. Make sure to leave sufficient space between the cheeses. And don't forget to oil the wooden boards before packing them away so they will be ready for the next time.

CANDIED WALNUTS

Makes 200g

200G SHELLED WALNUTS

100G SUGAR

¾ TSP SEA SALT

First line a baking tray with parchment paper and spread the walnuts on top. Place the sugar in a medium saucepan over a moderate heat until the edges begin to melt. Swirl the liquefied sugar around the saucepan carefully and continue to cook until the sugar is caramel coloured. Remove from the heat, quickly sprinkle over the salt, swirl, then pour over the walnuts in the baking tray. Be careful as the caramel will be scalding hot! Leave to cool. Once cold, break apart and keep in a sealed jar until ready to serve.

APPLE CRISPS

These are very moreish so make as many as you like – sure its a healthy treat!

5 APPLES, WASHED AND VERY THINLY SLICED

1 TSP CINNAMON

Preheat the oven to 160°C/fan 140°C/gas 2. Line a baking tray with parchment paper. Place the thinly sliced apples on the tray, sprinkle over the cinnamon and bake for about 35 to 40 minutes or until golden brown and crisp. Allow to cool completely before serving or sealing in an airtight container.

FARMHOUSE FESTIVITIES

Christmas at Ballyknochen

Christmas is always the most important celebration in our farmhouse. There have been some years when the decorations were put up at the beginning of November, as we were staging photos, and we left them up, much to the delight of the children. Talk about Christmas coming early! As our B&B now closes in the first week in December for weekend guests, it's become a habit to decorate early for Christmas.

Ballyknocken Bay, Thyme and Cranberry Christmas Turkey with Bacon Stuffing Balls

Serves 8 to 10

My claim to fame is that I'm a decent turkey plucker, having spent many hours helping my mother prepare turkeys for the Christmas market when she closed the B&B for the winter months.

FOR THE BASTING MIX

100ML CRANBERRY JUICE

4 TBSP LIGHT BROWN SUGAR

1 TBSP WHOLEGRAIN MUSTARD

2 TSP CHOPPED THYME

FRESHLY GROUND BLACK PEPPER

RAPESEED OIL, FOR ROASTING

4.5KG OVEN-READY TURKEY, GIBLETS AND NECK REMOVED

2 TBSP BUTTER, MELTED

SALT AND FRESHLY GROUND BLACK PEPPER

1 ONION, SLICED IN HALF, FOR THE CAVITY

1 LARGE SPRIG OF BAY LEAVES, FOR THE CAVITY

1 LEMON, CUT IN HALF, FOR THE CAVITY

2 TSP THYME, CHOPPED

Preheat the oven to 200°C/fan 180°C/ gas 6.

Put all the ingredients for the basting mix into a small saucepan, bring to the boil and simmer over a medium to low heat for about 10 minutes until it thickens slightly. Set aside and let it cool.

Calculate the cooking time for the turkey. This will be 25 to 30 minutes per kg plus an extra 30 minutes, and it will need a resting time of 30 minutes. So, for a 4.5kg bird, you'll need to put it in the oven 2 hrs 50 mins to 3 hrs 15 mins before you want to eat.

Pour some oil into a foil tray liner in a roasting tray. Place the turkey, breast side up, into the tray. Brush with the melted butter and season with salt and freshly ground black pepper.

Put the onion, bay leaves and lemon into the cavity and spoon in about 4 tbsp of the basting mix. Pour half of the rest of the basting mix over the turkey and sprinkle over the chopped thyme. Place in the preheated oven and baste every 30 minutes. Use foil to cover the turkey if it is browning too fast.

FOR THE STUFFING BALLS

RAPESEED OIL, FOR FRYING

200G DICED SMOKED BACON

2 ONIONS, VERY FINELY CHOPPED

2 CELERY STICKS, FINELY CHOPPED

2 GARLIC CLOVES, FINELY CHOPPED

300G FRESH BREADCRUMBS

3 TBSP DRIED CRANBERRIES, FINELY CHOPPED

$1\frac{1}{2}$ TSP CHOPPED SAGE

1 TBSP CHOPPED PARSLEY

2 FREE-RANGE EGGS, BEATEN

SALT AND FRESHLY GROUND BLACK PEPPER

SPRIGS OF BAY LEAF, TO GARNISH

5 SPRIGS OF THYME, TO GARNISH

To prepare the stuffing balls, heat a large frying pan with some oil over a medium heat and fry the bacon until crispy. Using a slotted spoon, remove from the pan, drain on kitchen paper and set aside. Add the onions and celery to the pan and sauté until softened but not browned. This will take about 5 to 6 minutes. Add the garlic and cook for 1 minute.

Remove from the heat and stir in the breadcrumbs, cranberries, sage, parsley, salt and freshly ground black pepper. Add the crispy bacon and the beaten eggs. Mix well and, with wet hands, shape into balls.

Heat some oil in a large frying pan. Add the stuffing balls in batches, brown and heat through, then remove and keep warm.

To serve the turkey, when rested, unwrap the foil and place the bird on a large, warm platter. Pile the stuffing balls on the side. Garnish with bay leaves and thyme sprigs. Serve with Garlic and Rosemary Roast Potatoes (see p. 136).

Festive Baked Ham

Serves 6 to 8

A baked ham is very versatile and not only for Christmas – they're great for communion luncheons or even Easter feasts and I'm partial to ham with cabbage, champ and parsley sauce. But I'm very fussy: the cabbage must be just cooked, not over cooked, the champ perfectly seasoned and I like onions in my parsley sauce – I did say I was fussy!

4.5KG HAM ON THE BONE, PREFERABLY LIGHTLY SMOKED, SOAKED OVERNIGHT

1 ONION, PEELED

2 CARROTS, PEELED AND ROUGHLY CHOPPED

3 BAY LEAVES

5 TO 6 CLOVES

10 TO 12 BLACK PEPPERCORNS

2 CINNAMON STICKS

600ML CIDER

ABOUT 3 LITRES WATER

FOR THE GLAZE

60G DARK BROWN SUGAR

100G MAPLE SYRUP

2 TSP WHOLEGRAIN MUSTARD

1 ORANGE, JUICE AND ZEST

3 TO 4 MEDIUM ORANGES, PEELED AND SLICED THINLY, TO DECORATE

CLOVES, TO INSERT

8 STAR ANISE

Weigh the ham before you begin to cook. The cooking time for ham is 20 minutes for every 500g, so a 4.5kg ham will need to cook for 3 hours.

Place the ham, onion, carrots, bay leaves, cloves, peppercorns and cinnamon sticks in a large saucepan. Add the cider and enough cold water to cover the ham. Bring to the boil and simmer according to the calculated cooking time. Keep topping up the water level and scooping the foam off the top as needed.

In the meantime, mix all the ingredients for the glaze and set aside.

Carefully remove the ham from the liquid. Preheat the oven to 200°C/fan 180°C/gas 6. Lift the ham into a large roasting tin. Cut away the skin leaving an even layer of fat. Score the layer of fat in a diamond pattern and spread some of the glaze over the top.

Roast in the oven for 10 minutes. Then arrange the orange slices over the top, inserting them with cloves. Add the star anise in between the orange slices. Spread on some more glaze and roast for a further 20 minutes, until the oranges are golden.

Leave to rest, covered, for 20 minutes before carving.

Individual Black Forest Trifles

Makes 4 to 5 glasses, depending on the size

It's not Christmas at Ballyknocken without trifle. Here's my twist on the classic, inspired by my year spent living in the deep south of Germany, where the freshly made Schwarzwälder Kirschtorte (Black Forest Gateau) was a real treat.

400G PITTED CHERRIES IN SYRUP, DRAINED AND SYRUP RETAINED

3 TSP ARROWROOT, TO THICKEN

100G DARK CHOCOLATE (70% COCOA SOLIDS)

150G MASCARPONE

400ML CREAM, LIGHTLY WHIPPED

KIRSCH OR BRANDY, TO TASTE

8 SLICES CHOCOLATE LOAF CAKE OR BROWNIE, ROUGHLY CHOPPED

CHERRIES, TO DECORATE

In a small saucepan, mix about 100ml of the cherry syrup with the arrowroot. Place over a medium heat and stir until it thickens. Set aside.

Melt the chocolate by placing in a ceramic bowl over a saucepan of simmering water. When melted, set aside half. When cooled, carefully mix the other half with the mascarpone, 200ml of the whipped cream and kirsch or brandy to taste.

To flavour the chocolate cake, mix another 100ml of the cherry syrup with about 3 tbsp of kirsch. Lay the cake slices on a plate and pour this mix over, allowing it to soak in.

To assemble, place some pretty glasses on a small tray. Place 3 or 4 cherries into each glass. Spoon in some chocolate mascarpone cream and add some pieces of the flavoured chocolate cake, followed by a good swirl of the thickened cherry syrup and some of the remaining 200ml of whipped cream and, finally, a drizzle of the melted chocolate. Repeat these layers, ending with whipped cream, then transfer the tray to the fridge.

Remove from the fridge 20 minutes before you want to serve them. Spoon over a little cherry syrup and place a cherry on top of each trifle.

Ginger and Orange Christmas Pudding

Makes a 900ml pudding

In our house, when making the pudding, we keep the fantastic tradition of stirring – each family member has a go and makes a wish (usually about possible large Christmas gifts!) I've added ginger here for a tasty twist to this pudding and also to add another level to the festive flavours.

FOR STEEPING

100G RAISINS

100G SULTANAS

75G CURRANTS

3 TBSP MIXED PEEL

1 TBSP FINELY CHOPPED CRYSTALLISED GINGER

3 TBSP GRAND MARNIER (OR OTHER ORANGE LIQUEUR OR BRANDY)

100ML ORANGE JUICE

75G DARK BROWN SUGAR

MELTED BUTTER, FOR BRUSHING

50G GOLDEN CASTER SUGAR

3 TBSP GROUND ALMONDS

40G FRESH WHITE BREADCRUMBS

80G PLAIN FLOUR

½ TSP GROUND GINGER

½ ORANGE, ZEST ONLY

1 EGG, BEATEN

60G CHILLED BUTTER OR SUET, FINELY CHOPPED

Combine all the ingredients for steeping, cover and leave in a cool place overnight.

To make the pudding, generously brush a 900ml pudding bowl with melted butter. Line the base with a circle of parchment paper.

Mix the caster sugar, almonds, breadcrumbs, flour, ginger and orange zest together in a large bowl. Carefully stir the soaked fruit into the dry ingredients, then stir in the beaten egg. Finally, add the butter or suet.

Spoon the mixture into the pudding bowl. Then cover the bowl tightly with a well-fitting lid or a layer of parchment paper and foil. Secure with string, ensuring to cross the string over the top of the bowl. This forms a handle.

Place the bowl in a saucepan a quarter full of boiling water – the water should be only halfway up the sides of the pudding bowl – and reduce the heat. Cover and leave to simmer very gently for 4 hours – remember to top up with boiling water as required. Carefully remove the pudding from the saucepan, cool in the bowl and store in a cool, dry place.

FOR THE ORANGE SAUCE

100ML FRESH ORANGE JUICE

50ML CASTER SUGAR

1 TBSP BUTTER

ICING SUGAR, FOR DUSTING

4 TO 5 CRYSTALLISED GINGER PIECES, ROUGHLY CHOPPED, TO DECORATE

½ ORANGE, ZEST ONLY

To make the orange sauce, combine the orange juice and sugar in a small saucepan over a medium heat. Simmer for 12 minutes until thick. Whisk in the butter and cool. This will keep in the fridge overnight.

On Christmas Day, reheat the pudding by steaming again for at least 1½ hours.

Turn the pudding out and dust with icing sugar. Warm the orange sauce and decorate the pudding with ginger pieces and orange zest on top. (P.S. A dash of brandy in the orange sauce is nice too!)

INDEX

A

accompaniments, vegetables, 133
antipasti platter, 31–6
apples
    apple breakfast compote, 12
    apple cider sauce, 116
    apple crisps, 230
    apple jelly, 178
apricot and lemon balm yoghurt cake, 226
artichoke, mint and broad bean salad, 150
asparagus
    chargrilled, 37
    tomato haddock with asparagus and prosciutto, 76
Aunty Trina's tea brack, 218

B

bacon and broccoli frittata, 19
bacon stuffing balls, 234–6
baked ham, 238
baked oysters with bacon, 82
baked trout with fennel, lime and wasabi cream sauce, 78
Ballyknocken bay, thyme and cranberry Christmas turkey with bacon stuffing balls, 234–6
Ballyknocken dauphinoise, 134
Ballyknocken drop scones with blackberry sauce and orange mascarpone cream, 22
Ballyknocken garden salad with lemon and balsamic dressing, 33
Ballyknocken granola, 18
Ballyknocken House and Cookery School, 1–2
Ballyknocken Irish–Italian antipasti platter, 31–6
Ballyknocken soda seed bread, 208
Ballyknocken's famous rhubarb and ginger jam, 179
balsamic vinegar, 176
barley, shallot and spinach soup, 66
bay, thyme and cranberry Christmas turkey with bacon stuffing balls, 234–6
beef dishes
    beef and stout pies with potato pastry topping, 112–14

beef Wellington, 100
    cooking temperature for beef, 90
    peppered sirloin steak with whiskey cream sauce, 115
    Wicklow Wolf braised beef, 110
beetroot
    beetroot and prosciutto salad with orange dressing, 148
    beetroot soup, 60
berry pannacotta tart, 190
biscuits, oaty chive, 217
Black Forest trifles, 242
black pudding, 151
blackberries
    blackberry and rhubarb upside-down cake, 202
    blackberry dressing, 102–3
    blackberry sauce, 22
    Wicklow summer pudding, 204
    blackcurrant and rosemary fool, 194
blueberries
    lemonade, white chocolate and fraughan, 212
    Prosecco, lemon balm and blueberry jellies, 200
    very berry pannacotta tart, 190
boiled eggs, 6
borage flowers, 154
breads
    Ballyknocken soda seed, 208
    Mary's brown bread, 210
    soda farls, 209
breakfast
    Ballyknocken drop scones with blackberry sauce and orange mascarpone cream, 22
    Ballyknocken granola, 18
    eggs, 6, 9
    French toast with rose petal syrup, plums and goat's cheese, 24
    omelettes, 9
    orchard apple breakfast compote, 12
    porridge with cinammon and pear compote, 10
    rhubarb, orange and ginger compote, 14
    smoked bacon and broccoli frittata, 19
    spinach fritters with poached eggs and roast tomatoes, 20

broad bean, artichoke and mint salad, 150
broccoli
    broccoli and smoked bacon frittata, 19
    with wild garlic sauce, 144
brown bread, 210
butter
    celery seed and black olive, 224
    chilli, lime and cumin, 224
    flavoured, 133, 224
    how to make, 222
    sweet orange and cinnamon breakfast, 224

C
cabbage, 238
cakes
    apricot and lemon balm yoghurt, 226
    Aunty Trina's tea brack, 218
    blackberry and rhubarb upside-down, 202
    celebratory cheese, 228
    chocolate mousse, 188
see also desserts
candied walnuts, 230
cannellini beans, 68
caponata, Sicilian, 31
caramelised onions
    caramelised onion and leek scones, 216
    as side dish, 133
casserole, rabbit, 126
Catherine's favourite pesto, 169
cauliflower cheese bake, 140
celebratory cheese cake, 228
celery seed and black olive butter, 224
chard, rainbow, 146
chargrilled courgette salad with crumbled black
                pudding and chilli sauce, 151
chargrilling, meat, 93
cheese
    celebratory cheese cake, 228
    cheese sauce, 140
    cheeseboards, 230
    cheesy lemon cups with garlic herb oil, 50
chicken dishes
    chicken hotpot, 106
    chicken liver parfait, 42
    chicken stock, 58
    chicken supreme with spinach and herb stuffing
        and sorrel sauce, 104–5
    cooking temperature, 90
    Sicilian lemony roast, 108
chilli, lime and cumin butter, 224

chocolate mint liqueur, 168
chocolate mousse cake, 188
choux pastry, 192
Christmas dishes
    Ballyknocken bay, thyme and cranberry Christmas
        turkey with bacon stuffing balls, 234–6
    festive baked ham, 238
    ginger and orange Christmas
        pudding, 244–6
    individual Black Forest trifles, 242
    chutney, plum and red onion, 182
ciabatta, herb, 54
cinammon and pear compote, 10
cinnamon pear preserve, 180
compotes
    cinnamon and pear, 10
    orchard apple breakfast, 12
    rhubarb, orange and ginger, 14
cooking
    fish, 72–5
    meat, 90–3
crab and Dillisk mini-tartlets, 40
creams
    lemon verbena, 186
    orange mascarpone, 22
    sorrel cream, 104–5
    wasabi cream sauce, 78
    whiskey cream, 115
    creamy mushroom and pink peppercorn sauce, 118
crisps, apple, 230
croquettes, ham, 120
croutons, 133
curing, salmon, 75
curried mussel soup, 64

D
dates, stuffed, 118
desserts
    blackberry and rhubarb upside-down cake, 202
    blackcurrant and rosemary fool, 194
    chocolate mousse cake, 188
    elderflower fritters, 187
    gooseberry and elderflower fool, 194
    lemon meringue pie, 198
    Mary's Eve's pudding with lemon verbena cream, 186
    mini strawberry and lemon eclairs, 192
    Prosecco, lemon balm and blueberry jellies, 200
    very berry pannacotta tart, 190
    Wicklow summer pudding, 204
dill and strawberry salad, 38

Dillisk and crab mini-tartlets, 40
dips
    tahini yoghurt dressing, 225
    tomato, 54
dressings
    blackberry, 102–3
    herb, 150
    honey and apple yoghurt, 225
    honey and ginger yoghurt, 225
    lemon and balsamic, 33
    orange, 148
    strawberry, 154
    tahini yoghurt, 225
drop scones with blackberry sauce and orange
        mascarpone cream, 22
duck breasts, five-spice, 124

E
easy mackerel pâté, 44
éclairs, lemon and strawberry, 192
eggs, 6, 9, 20, 37
elderflower fritters, 187
Eve's pudding with lemon verbena cream, 186

F
farls, 209
festive baked ham, 238
fig and olive tapenade, 32
fish dishes
    baked oysters with bacon, 82
    baked trout with fennel, lime and wasabi
        cream sauce, 78
    grilling fish, 75
    hot smoking salmon, 75
    Irish seafood risotto, 86
    Murrough posh fish pie, 84
    pan-frying fish, 72
    roasting fish, 72
    smoked salmon and salmon fish cakes, 79
    tomato haddock with asparagus and prosciutto, 76
five-spice seared duck breasts, 124
flattened toasted herb ciabatta, 54
flavoured butters, 133, 224
flavoured salts, 170
fools
    blackcurrant and rosemary, 194
    gooseberry and elderflower, 194
fraughans, 212
freezing, vegetables, 130

French sorrel, 62, 104–5
French toast with rose petal syrup, plums and goat's
        cheese, 24
fried eggs, 9
frittata, smoked bacon and broccoli, 19
fritters
    elderflower, 187
    spinach, 20
fruit
    apple jelly, 178
    Ballyknocken's famous rhubarb and ginger jam, 179
    cinnamon pear preserve, 180
    fruit jelly, 200
    marsala pear relish, 183
    plum and red onion chutney, 182
    strawberry and balsamic jam, 176
frying, meat, 93

G
garlic and rosemary roast potatoes, 136
garlic herb oil, 50
garlic sauce, 144
ginger and orange Christmas pudding, 244–6
goat's cheese, 24
gooseberry and elderflower fool, 194
granola, Ballyknocken, 18
gravy
    caramelised onions, 133
    shallot and red wine, 96–8
    Wicklow Wolf braised beef, 110
grilling, fish, 75

H
haddock, tomato, 76
ham
    festive baked ham, 238
    ham croquettes with leek and paprika sauce, 120
hazelnut and stuffed date pork fillet, 118
herbs
    Catherine's favourite pesto, 169
    chocolate mint liqueur, 168
    growing in jars, 162
    herb ciabatta, 54
    herb dressing, 150
    herb oil, 50, 133
    herb salts, 170
    herb syrups, 166
    herby Parmesan-encrusted rack of lamb, 94
honey, red wine and juniper red cabbage, 141

honey and apple yoghurt dressing, 225
honey and ginger yoghurt dressing, 225
honey and raspberry sauce, 124
hot smoking, salmon, 75
hotpot, chicken, 106
hummus, 32

I

Irish seafood risotto, 86
Irish–Italian antipasti platter, 31–6
Italian-style tomato, shallot and rosemary chicken
    hotpot, 106

J

jam
    Ballyknocken's famous rhubarb and ginger, 179
    making, 172
    strawberry and balsamic, 176
jars
    growing herbs in, 162
    sterilising, 133, 172
    jelly, apple, 178
Jerusalem artichoke soup, 60

K

kale, cannellini and potato soup, 68

L

lamb
    cooking temperatures, 90
    herby Parmesan-encrusted rack of Wicklow lamb, 94
    Lamb Wellington with wild garlic, 100
    leg of Wicklow lamb with Moroccan mint jelly and
        shallot and red wine gravy, 96–8
    marinade, 102–3
    Wicklow lamb steak with wild leaves, mushrooms
        and a blackberry dressing, 102–3
leek
    leek and paprika sauce, 120
    roasted red pepper, leek and farmhouse cheese
        terrine, 46
lemon
    cheesy lemon cups, 50
    lemon and balsamic dressing, 33
    lemon and strawberry éclairs, 192
    lemon balm and apricot yoghurt cake, 226
    lemon hummus, 32

lemon meringue pie, 198
lemon verbena cream, 186
lemonade, white chocolate and fraughan scones, 212
liqueur, chocolate mint, 168

M

mackerel pâté, 44
mangetout, Wicklow Blue cheese and borage flower
    salad, 154
Marie Rose sauce, 41
marinade, lamb, 102–3
marsala pear relish, 183
Mary's brown bread, 210
Mary's Eve's pudding with lemon verbena cream, 186
mash
    mustard and spinach, 135
    sweet potato, 84
    mayonnaise, tarragon, 37
meat dishes
    beef and stout pies with potato pastry topping, 112–14
    chargrilling, 93
    chicken supreme with spinach and herb
        stuffing, 104–5
    five-spice seared duck breasts, 124
    frying, 93
    ham croquettes with leek and paprika sauce, 120
    how to cook meat, 90–3
    Italian-style tomato, shallot and rosemary chicken
        hotpot, 106
    Lamb Wellington with wild garlic, 100
    leg of Wicklow lamb with Moroccan mint jelly and
        shallot and red wine gravy, 96–8
    peppered sirloin steak with whiskey cream sauce, 115
    poaching, 93
    roasting, 90
    rosemary, apple and celery-stuffed pork chops, 116
    rosemary venison with shallot and red wine sauce, 122
    Sicilian lemony roast chicken and potatoes, 108
    stir-frying, 93
    stuffed date and hazelnut pork fillet, 118
    Wicklow lamb steak with wild leaves, mushrooms
        and a blackberry dressing, 102–3
    Wicklow rack of lamb, herby Parmesan-encrusted, 94
    Wicklow Wolf braised beef, 110
    winter rabbit casserole, 126
Mediterranean omelette, 9
meringue pie, lemon, 198
mini strawberry and lemon éclairs, 192
mini-tartlets, Dillisk and crab, 40
mint, artichoke and broad bean salad, 150

mint jelly, Moroccan, 96–8
Murrough posh fish pie, 84
mussel soup, curried, 64
mustard and spinach mash, 135

O

oaty chive biscuits, 217
oil, herb-infused, 155
olive and fig tapenade, 32
omelettes, 9
onions
    caramelised, 133
    onion, leek and pancetta tart, 34
    plum and red onion chutney, 182
orange
    orange, rhubarb and ginger compote, 14
    orange and ginger Christmas pudding, 244–6
    orange dressing, 148
    orange mascarpone cream, 22
orchard apple breakfast compote, 12
oysters, baked, 82

P

pak choi, 124
pan-frying, fish, 72
pannacotta tart, 190
parfait, chicken liver, 42
parsnips, polenta and parsley, 138
passata, tomatoes, 133
pâté, mackerel, 44
pear
    marsala pear relish, 183
    pear and cinnamon compote, 10
    pear and shallot tarte tatin, 156
    pear preserve, 180
    peppered sirloin steak with whiskey cream sauce, 115
pestos
    Catherine's favourite, 169
    lemon and chilli, 54
pickling, vegetables, 130
pies, beef and stout, 112–14
platter, antipasti, 31–6
plums
    French toast with rose petal syrup, plums and goat's
        cheese, 24
    plum and red onion chutney, 182
    plum salsa, 94
poaching
    eggs, 9, 20

meat, 93
polenta and parsley chunky parsnips, 138
pork dishes
    bacon and broccoli frittata, 19
    bacon stuffing balls, 234–6
    cooking temperature, 90
    rosemary, apple and celery-stuffed pork chops, 116
    stuffed date and hazelnut pork fillet, 118
porridge with cinnamon and pear compote, 10
potatoes
    Ballyknocken dauphinoise, 134
    garlic and rosemary roast potatoes, 136
    mustard and spinach mash, 135
    potato and Parmesan topping, 106
    potato pastry topping, 112–14
    sweet potato, 84
prawn skewers, 41
preserve, cinnamon pear, 180
prosciutto, 76, 148
Prosecco, lemon balm and blueberry jellies, 200
puddings
    black pudding, 151
    ginger and orange Christmas pudding, 244–6
    Mary's Eve's pudding with lemon verbena cream, 186
    pudding with lemon verbena cream, 186
    tomato and basil summer puddings, 158
see also desserts
purple sprouting broccoli with wild garlic sauce, 144

R

rabbit casserole, 126
rack of Wicklow lamb, 94
rainbow chard with garlic and blue cheese, 146
raspberries
    very berry pannacotta tart, 190
    Wicklow summer pudding, 204
red cabbage, 141
red peppers, roasted, 46
relish, marsala pear, 183
rhubarb
    blackberry and rhubarb upside-down cake, 202
    rhubarb, orange and ginger compote, 14
    rhubarb and ginger jam, 179
risotto, Irish seafood, 86
roasting
    fish, 72
    meat, 90
red peppers, 46
rose petal syrup, 24
rosemary, apple and celery-stuffed pork chops, 116

rosemary and garlic roast potatoes, 136

rosemary and lemon salt, 170

rosemary venison with shallot and red wine sauce, 122

S

salads

Ballyknocken garden, 33

beetroot and prosciutto, 148

chargrilled courgette, 151

mangetout, Wicklow Blue cheese and borage flower, 154

mint, artichoke and broad bean, 150

the perfect salad, 133

Scotch egg, 37

smoked salmon roll, 52

smoked trout, dill and strawberry, 38

salmon

hot smoking, 75

smoked salmon and salmon fish cakes, 79

smoked salmon roll salad, 52

salsas

plum, 94

for roasted red pepper, leek and soft farmhouse cheese terrine, 46

salts, 170

sauces

apple cider, 116

blackberry, 22

cheese, 140

creamy mushroom and pink peppercorn, 118

homemade tomato, 31

honey and raspberry, 124

leek and paprika, 120

Marie Rose, 41

shallot and red wine, 122

sorrel cream, 104–5

wasabi cream, 78

whiskey cream, 115

wild garlic, 144

scones

caramelised onion and leek, 216

drop, 22

lemonade, white chocolate and fraughan, 212

Scotch egg salad with tarragon mayonnaise, rocket and chargrilled asparagus, 37

scrambled eggs, 6

seafood risotto, 86

seaweed, Dillisk, 40

shallots

shallot, spinach and barley soup, 66

shallot and pear tarte tatin, 156

shallot and red wine gravy, 96–8

shallot and red wine sauce, 122

Sicilian caponata, 31

Sicilian lemony roast chicken and potatoes, 108

side dishes

Ballyknocken dauphinoise, 134

cauliflower cheese bake, 140

garlic and rosemary roast potatoes, 136

honey, red wine and juniper red cabbage, 141

individual tomato and basil summer puddings, 158

mustard and spinach mash, 135

pan-fried rainbow chard with garlic and blue cheese, 146

polenta and parsley chunky parsnips, 138

purple sprouting broccoli with garlic butter, 144

shallot and pear tarte tatin, 156

sirloin steak, peppered, 115

smoked bacon and broccoli frittata, 19

smoked salmon and salmon fish cakes, 79

smoked salmon roll salad, 52

smoked trout, dill and strawberry salad, 38

soda farls, 209

soda seed bread, 208

sorrel, wild garlic and potato soup, 62

sorrel cream sauce, 104–5

soups

beetroot, 60

curried mussel, 64

Jerusalem artichoke with bacon, 60

kale, cannellini and potato, 68

shallot, spinach and barley, 66

sorrel, wild garlic and potato, 62

vegetable and chicken stock, 58

Spanish omelette, 9

spinach

spinach, barley and shallot soup, 66

spinach and herb stuffing, 104–5

spinach and mustard mash, 135

spinach fritters with poached eggs and roast tomatoes, 20

starters

Ballyknocken garden salad with lemon and balsamic dressing, 33

Ballyknocken Irish–Italian antipasti platter, 31–6

chargrilled prawn skewers with Marie Rose sauce, 41

cheesy lemon cups with garlic herb oil, 50

chicken liver parfait, 42

crab and Dillisk mini-tartlets, 40

easy mackerel pâté, 44

fig and olive tapenade, 32

flattened toasted herb ciabatta, 54

lemon hummus, 32
onion, leek and pancetta tart, 34
roasted red pepper, leek and soft farmhouse cheese terrine, 46
Scotch egg salad with tarragon mayonnaise, rocket and chargrilled asparagus, 37
Sicilian caponata, 31
smoked salmon roll salad, 52
smoked trout, dill and strawberry salad, 38
tomato, yoghurt and lemon-and-chilli pesto pots, 54
sterilising, jars, 133, 172
stir-frying, meat, 93
stock, vegetable and chicken, 58
stock syrups, 166
strawberries
    strawberry and balsamic jam, 176
    strawberry and dill salad, 38
    strawberry and lemon éclairs, 192
    strawberry dressing, 154
    Wicklow summer pudding, 204
stuffed date and hazelnut pork fillet, 118
summer puddings
    tomato and basil, 158
    Wicklow, 204
    sweet orange and cinnamon breakfast butter, 224
sweet potato, mashed, 84
syrups, 166

T

tahini yoghurt dressing, 225
tapenade, olive and fig, 32
tarragon mayonnaise, 37
tarts
    Dillisk and crab mini-tartlets, 40
    onion, leek and pancetta, 34
    tarte tatin, shallot and pear, 156
    very berry pannacotta, 190
    tea brack, 218
    terrine, roasted red pepper, 46
    thyme and chilli salt, 170
toast, French, 24
tomatoes
    homemade tomato sauce, 31
    roasted, 20, 76
    tomato, shallot and rosemary chicken hotpot, 106
    tomato, yoghurt and lemon-and-chilli pesto pots, 54
    tomato and basil summer puddings, 158
    tomato haddock with asparagus and prosciutto, 76
    tomato passata, 133
trifles, Black Forest, 242

trout
    baked, 78
    smoked, 38
turkey with bacon stuffing balls, 234–6

U

upside-down cake, blackberry and rhubarb, 202

V

vegetables
    accompaniments, 133
    caramelised onions, 133
    freezing, 130
    pickling, 130
    sterilising, 133
    stock, 58
    tomato passata, 133
    see also side dishes
venison, rosemary, 122
very berry pannacotta tart, 190

W

walnuts, candied, 230
wasabi cream sauce, 78
whiskey cream sauce, 115
Wicklow Blue, 154, 180
Wicklow lamb
    herby Parmesan-encrusted rack with plum salsa, 94
    leg with Moroccan mint jelly and shallot and red wine gravy, 96–8
    steak with wild leaves, mushrooms and a blackberry dressing, 102–3
Wicklow summer pudding, 204
Wicklow Wolf braised beef, 110
winter rabbit casserole, 126

Y

yoghurt
    apricot and lemon balm yoghurt cake, 226
    honey and apple yoghurt dressing, 225
    honey and ginger yoghurt dressing, 225
    how to make, 222
    tahini yoghurt dressing, 225